Charl

Mom and Dad

PRAYER--
ITS DEEPER DIMENSIONS

PRAYER--
ITS DEEPER DIMENSIONS

A CHRISTIAN LIFE Symposium
with chapters contributed by

Alan Redpath • *Paris Reidhead*

J. Edwin Orr • *Bramwell Tripp*

Armin R. Gesswein • *Rosalind Rinker*

Clifford H. Richmond • *Samuel M. Shoemaker*

Norman P. Grubb • *Leonard Ravenhill*

Donald E. Hoke • *Gladys M. Rose*

A. W. Tozer

ZONDERVAN PUBLISHING HOUSE
Grand Rapids, Michigan

CONTENTS

1. WHAT IS PRAYER?

by Alan Redpath
Pastor, Moody Memorial Church, Chicago

Deep in your heart, do you admit that your prayer life lacks power? Do you rise from your knees weary instead of refreshed? Does your desire for intimate fellowship with God go unsatisfied?

Do not despair. This may be an indication that the Holy Spirit is calling you to a true knowledge of prayer — prayer that takes hold of God's strength and witnesses His power in action.

This is the true purpose of prayer — to enable us to set the supernatural power of God at work in overcoming the natural problems and situations of life.

Two steps are necessary so that we realize this purpose for ourselves.

First, have you completely committed yourself to Christ, allowing the Holy Spirit to fill you? If so, you may enter into a thrilling life of prayer, the dimensions of which you have never before known.

Second, you must know what true prayer is, what it can do.

Is it a spiritual exercise, a channel for asking God to fulfill your desires? No. Nor is it even enough to say that prayer is communion with God.

At its highest and best, prayer is a weapon — the most powerful weapon a Christian has in a world where evil often seems to triumph. Used by ordinary people like you

7

and me it can turn the scales in favor of a hopelessly weak minority, in the most impossible of situations.

Let us turn to the Bible to see what this means. The twelfth chapter of Acts provides a tremendous insight into the great warfare of Christian life.

The first four verses give us a picture of evil triumphant. The powerful, the ruthless Herod the Great had determined to crush the apostles. James has been killed. Peter has been cast into the inmost prison to await death.

As I read this passage, with the ears of my soul I hear the echo of one iron gate after another bang behind Peter. Finally he is flung into the darkness of the innermost prison, chained between two soldiers. Surely this is the end. There can be no escape.

Do you know something of Peter's experience? Your prison walls perhaps have not been made of granite or of stone. The gates have not been made of iron. But you have been in such a dark dungeon spiritually that you are completely shut in and baffled.

Every door has shut in your face. It has been disappointment and misunderstanding and rebuff. Nobody understands your need and situation. It has been bang, bang, bang, one door after another, and you are deep in the inmost prison today, shut in to yourself and away from God.

Now, what can prayer do? Peter's jailers had closed every door they could, but there was one door they couldn't shut — a door leading straight up to heaven.

"Peter therefore was kept in prison: but prayer was made without ceasing of the church unto God for him" (Acts 12:5).

The way through to Peter in his prison was barred — sixteen soldiers, two chains, three gates, Herod's grim determination to have him out shortly and kill him. On the horizontal level, there was no way through to Peter in that prison.

There's no way through to where you are either, on the horizontal level. No way of escape, no way out. No one who can come to help, no one who understands. No one who has the answer to your need. No one who can set you free from those chains. That's the situation in which you find yourself. There is no way out.

But there is a way you can be reached on the vertical level. "But prayer was made without ceasing of the church unto God for him."

What was the character of the prayer that got this man out, that turned the scale?

It was persistent praying, prayer without ceasing.

It was prevailing praying. It was made "of the church." Not just one person but the whole church was involved in this.

It was pointed praying. It was made "unto God" like an arrow shot up to the very throne of God.

It was personal praying. "It was for him."

What could a little handful of Christian people do in a situation like that? They could pass resolutions and make a petition to Herod. That would do a lot of good! They could raise some money to blow the prison up. How futile!

There rings in my soul a consciousness of my own helplessness apart from learning to pray like this. What can a little group of Christian people do to clean up not only the face of a city but to change its heart? Nothing. What can we do to help the world get out of its prison? Nothing.

What can I do to get out of my own prison? Nothing. What can you do when you are the victim of satanic power? What can you do, ultimately, to deliver yourself? Absolutely nothing. There is but one way of approach. It is persistent, prevailing, pointed, personal praying.

How does God answer? First of all, in a human sense, it
was late when Peter's answer came. This man's deliverance
was delayed to the last moment. Verse six tells us that it was
the same night "when Herod would have brought him
forth."

Day after day had passed by and prayer apparently
remained unanswered, and the last night had come. Why
didn't God step in and save Peter from that situation sooner?
I suggest that God wanted to teach the disciples a few
lessons about prayer, to teach Peter a few lessons about trust.

How wonderfully they all passed the test. The church
kept on praying. They didn't give in. They held on. Have
you prayed for many years for an unconverted friend or
loved one? Don't give up. God's delays are never God's
denials. The church kept on praying.

The church passed the test, and Peter passed the test
too. What does the sixth verse say? "Peter was . . . pan-
icking"? No. "Peter was . . . lying awake worrying about
his head coming off in the morning"? No. What was he
doing? "Sleeping."

Perhaps Peter was the only Christian in Jerusalem who
slept that night. The rest of them were praying for him.
And here was the man who in a few hours was to be
beheaded, not very comfortable, with his coat off, his shoes
and girdle off, chained to soldiers on each side, lying down,
fast asleep.

How on earth did Peter manage to sleep in a situation like
that? I think, quite simply, that he was doing what the Lord
Jesus wants you and me to do in our prisons today. He was
resting on the promises of God. In John 21:18 the risen
Lord said to His beloved Simon. "Simon, when thou wast
young, thou girdedst thyself, and walkedst whither thou
wouldest: but when thou shalt be old, thou shalt stretch
forth thy hands, and another shall gird thee."

In prison that night Peter must have reminded himself of that interview: "Lord, You said that to me a month or so ago. I am not old now. Herod says he is going to chop my head off tomorrow but how can he do that, for You have told me that one day I am going to grow old? I don't know how You are going to deliver me, but this I know, I am going to rest on the promises and have a good sleep." What a day it would be in your life if you could only put the Book right down in your heart and rest on its promises. Perhaps that is why you are in your prison. Perhaps that is why there is no escape yet, because in that prison the Lord is asking you now just to rest in the Word.

Peter wrote later on when he was old, "Now let us learn to cast all our cares upon him for he careth for you." In J. B. Phillips' *Letters to Young Churches,* the admonition is translated this way, "You can rest the weight of all your anxieties upon Him for you are always in His care."

Imprisoned soul, just listen to that and go on from here with your heart light. Leave the burden at the feet of the Lord Jesus. Hurl it at His feet. This is not being extreme or fanatical. It is taking the Word of God for what God intends it to be.

Here is the second fact about God's plan of deliverance: Notice how majestically the angel went about delivering Peter. Look at the eighth verse of this chapter. "The angel said unto him, Gird thyself (get dressed) and bind on thy sandals (put your shoes on and fasten them up). And so he did. And he saith unto him, Cast thy garment about thee (put on your coat), and follow me."

There follows the most leisurely procession out of a prison that I have ever heard of. The two soldiers were still sound asleep. Peter and the angel go through the inner ward, then another ward. The sixteen soldiers are around

somewhere, but they go past them. The iron gate opened
of its own accord as they came up to it, and Peter was free.

What the Scripture says is always true, "He that believeth
shall not make haste." And the law of God's working, my
beloved Christian friend, is "ye shall not go out with haste,
nor go by flight, for the Lord will go before you."

You and I are impatient to get out of these prisons. No one
is more impatient than I am to get a move on, to see
things happen and see God work. We have got to learn
what it is to regulate our pace to the slow, steady, majestic
movement of God. God is never in a hurry.

God's deliverance of Peter was not only late and leisurely.
It was limited. The tenth verse closes by telling us that
"forthwith the angel departed from him." In other words,
as soon as possible, Peter was left to act for himself.

Peter couldn't have gotten through iron gates without
a miracle, but he could certainly find his way to Mary's
house without a miracle. Have you learned this; that God
never does anything for you that you can do for yourself?
Of course, all our doing is His Spirit working in us, but He
expects us to use our brains, our judgment, our reason.

Jesus raised Lazarus from the tomb. Only God could do
a thing like that, but other people could loose him and
let him go.

Peter eventually arrives at Mary's house where there is an
all-night prayer meeting going on — for him, of course.
A damsel named Rhoda answers Peter's knock. Then she
runs to tell the others that it is Peter — with such terrific
excitement that she neglects to let him in.

An iron gate had opened of its own accord but a little
cottage door remained shut. How extraordinary!

The company said, "It can't be. It is his ghost, his angel."
As that dispute went on, poor Peter just kept on knocking,

"and when they opened the door and saw him, they were astonished."

Let's not rebuke them too harshly. Haven't you prayed like that too? How often the Lord has come knocking at the door and we have kept the door shut because we have been disputing and wrangling and discussing and questioning and asking, and He has gone away. How much of the wealth of God's grace have we missed simply because we didn't expect Him to answer when we prayed?

But Peter continued knocking. I see here in that simple little phrase the fulfillment at last of some evidences of Pentecost having really gripped him. Was this impetuous, hot-headed Peter? He wasn't angry. He just went on knocking.

In your life perhaps some great iron doors have swung open wonderfully in answer to prayer, yet there are little doors that seem to remain tight shut. Somehow you have stood knocking at the door of fellowship, friendship and love, and in some places it has been kept shut in your face. People perhaps haven't trusted you, have suspected your motives, and they have kept the door shut. If there are such doors still shut in your life, may I ask you to follow Peter's example and just continue knocking?

An angel of the Lord will knock at your door or come into your prison one morning. He will touch you and your chains will fall off, and with leisurely, majestic tread he will take you through a cold iron gate that leads to a city, the streets of which are pure gold. When you get there your eyes will behold a King, the One who is as the sun shining in His strength. Then you will know that our Lord Jesus has delivered you and brought you through every door, every prison, every dark and lonely valley and delivered you into His lovely presence forever and ever.

2. DO YOU PRAY IN FAITH?

by PARIS REIDHEAD

Pastor, Gospel Tabernacle of New York City
(First Christian and Missionary Alliance Church)

"I was particularly struck with the fact that the prayers that I had listened to, from week to week, were not, that I could see, answered. Indeed, I understood from their utterances in prayer, and from other remarks in their meetings, that those who offered them did not regard them as answered."

Such was the reaction of young, confused Charles G. Finney, later to become the nineteenth century's greatest evangelist, to the arid prayers of a group of Christians.

"This inconsistency," Finney wrote, "the fact that they prayed so much and were not answered, was a sad stumbling block to me. I knew not what to make of it."

Like Finney, are you troubled by the obvious absence of answers to the prayers of Christians today? More particularly, do you want to know, "Why aren't my prayers answered?"

You are not satisfied with prayer as merely a spiritual exercise to make you "feel better." You want nothing less than recognizable evidence of God's supernatural power at work in the world in answer to your petitions.

God *does* answer prayer today. If you are truly seeking after spiritual reality, you can unlock the door to this power.

God surely answered prayer in a supernatural way in the New Testament days. In fact, it was through answered prayer that the Lord Jesus Christ established proof of His

14

Person and mission in the world. He declared He was the Son of God. People came to Him with needs. They expected Him — if He were indeed what He claimed to be — to answer their requests. Christ prayed, His Heavenly Father answered and some — at least 500 to whom He ministered — believed on Him.

After Christ's resurrection people believed the disciples' claims about seeing Him alive because their prayers in His name were answered. More believed on Christ then than had believed during the days of His earthly ministry. Everywhere, during the first century, where the Gospel was preached, it was expected that prayer offered in the name of the Lord Jesus would be answered.

Because God answered prayer, a handful of humble believers was able to do what the Church has been unable to do in the last four centuries since the time of the Reformation.

Why aren't church members today more concerned about the absence of answers to their prayers? They rationalize this lack of power in various ways.

Some say, "These promises are not for today. This is another dispensation."

Others smugly suggest that "the canon of Scripture is now complete, and God does not work in this way any longer."

Still others when they pray add the usual formula for unbelief, "If it be Thy will." Then if the prayer is answered, they can take credit for having been heard of heaven. If the prayer is not answered, they console themselves by repeating the usual excuse, "It just isn't God's will."

What is wrong with this formula? God's Word, the Bible, is the revelation of His will. Where God's Word speaks, God's will is known. Before we pray we should search the Scriptures for the revelation of His will in the area about which we are praying.

It is ridiculous to suggest that someone pray, "Dear Lord, if it be Thy will, please bless this theft I am about to commit." God has spoken once for all and His will is known — "Thou shalt not steal."

On the other hand, if we are convinced we are praying in the Lord's will, it is sheer unbelief, or even worse, rebellion against the revealed will of God, to tack on the loophole, "If it be Thy will."

This is not to suggest that we should not recognize the will of God in prayer. In the Garden of Gethsemane, the Lord Jesus prayed, "Thy will be done." Likewise, when we are seeking guidance between two courses of action, we should pray, "Thy will be done."

The key to power in prayer is to follow the principles that are so simple, so clearly apparent in the Bible. These principles are not new. They were understood by the fathers of the Old Testament. Abraham faithfully observed them. Moses knew them and walked in the light of their blessing. They were familiar to Elijah and were understood by David. They are so simple that the humblest mind can discern them, so dynamic that nations were delivered and God's name marvelously glorified when they were employed.

First, you must enter into a right relationship with God. Abraham's understanding could not have been as complete as ours is. We have the whole of the Scriptures plus the fact that God has become flesh and dwelt among us to illustrate the implications of the wonderful privileges that are ours. We have the Holy Spirit, the Comforter, to empower us.

We who were sold under sin and bound in the fetters of unbelief have been redeemed, ransomed, regenerated. We who once were blind are made to see. We who once were dead are made alive. We who walked in darkness now walk in light. We who were the children of Satan now call an Almighty God, "Abba Father." We who once were powerless now have the power of the Holy Spirit.

The privilege of prayer is the birthright of the humblest child of God. We are exercising our right when we come before Him to "let your requests be made known unto God." Christ said, "Verily, verily, I say unto you, Whatsoever ye shall ask the Father in my name, he will give it you" (John 16:23).

Second, in your relationship as a child of God you must keep the channel of access to Him clear of sin and self.

His Word clearly states, "If I regard iniquity in my heart, the Lord will not hear me" (Psalm 66:18). God hates sin. If a child of His consents to hold unconfessed, unforgiven sin in his heart, his prayers will go unanswered.

"A conscience void of offence toward God and man" is a prerequisite to answered prayer. God has stated, "For thus saith the high and lofty One that inhabiteth eternity, whose name is Holy; I dwell in the high and holy place, with him also that is of a contrite and humble spirit, to revive the spirit of the humble, and to revive the heart of the contrite ones" (Isaiah 57:15). And again, "Who shall ascend into the hill of the Lord? or who shall stand in his holy place? He that hath clean hands, and a pure heart; who hath not lifted up his soul unto vanity, nor sworn deceitfully. He shall receive the blessing from the Lord, and righteousness from the God of his salvation" (Psalm 24:3-5).

Check your relationship to God and His Word to see where you have infringed upon His truths and thus kept God from answering prayer, rather than attributing the failure of answer to some change in the character of God.

If your relationship to God is proper, the Holy Spirit Himself will intercede for you according to the will of God (Romans 8:26, 27).

Third, you must pray in faith. "*Without faith it is impossible to please Him*" (Hebrews 11:6).

What is faith? It is simple confidence that, and this is stated reverently, "God is a gentleman who will keep His agreements and observe His contracts and fulfill His Word."

The Scripture states: "He that cometh to God must believe that he is . . ." (Hebrews 11:6). That He is what? That He is what He says He is, that He does what He says He will do. Faith is not measured by how much *you* have in God. Faith rests on the character of God, upon what God has revealed Himself to be. Faith is a gift from God, bestowed when we meet His conditions.

Psalm 9:10 says, "And they that know thy name will put their trust in thee: for thou, Lord, hast not forsaken them that seek thee." The Psalmist exhorted, "O magnify the Lord with me, and let us exalt his name together" (Psalm 34:3). As men of faith like David saw God exalted and magnified and saw the immensity of Him in all of His attributes, their hearts were stirred with wonder, awe and love. Little problems assumed their right relationship to His eternity, His infinity, His love, mercy and grace.

Get your eyes off yourself. Admit your failure and incapacity to accomplish anything of yourself. Bring your weary heart into the sanctuary where the secret of the Lord is and lie down and rest. Then shall you learn that "Great is the Lord, and greatly to be praised . . ." (Psalm 48:1). Then you will go forth in simple childlike confidence that the God who loved you, saved you, and whose you are is "mighty to save and strong to deliver."

What are the Bible principles of prayer? First, prayer is foundationed upon a right relationship to God, children coming to their father. Second, children who love their father will clear their lives of barriers to the expression of his love. Thirdly, children who have confidence in the character of their father believe that he will do what he says he will do.

In the Hebrides islands off the coast of Britain hungry men waited the Lord through long and lonely hours of the night for months at a time. Two godly women agonized in prayer for a revival in the churches of the Hebrides. They founded their confidence upon the fact that our God is a covenant-keeping God. And revival came. God gave to this generation, a little demonstration of what He can do and will do if there are a few who will "believe that He is, and that He is a rewarder of them that diligently seek Him."

If your prayers are not answered, do not rationalize their powerlessness. Admit honestly that you have not fully realized the implication of your relationship to your Heavenly Father. Instead of reflecting on God's character, examine your own and let the Holy Spirit unveil the attitudes and the actions which displease Him. Meditate upon the truths concerning our God until you see Him in all His glory.

Finally, ask the Holy Spirit to make the eternal principles of prayer vitally real in your life. Then shall your prayers be answered and the living Christ manifested in His resurrection glory.

3. POWER IN UNITED PRAYER

by J. Edwin Orr
Evangelist and Author

No great spiritual awakening has begun anywhere in the world apart from united prayer — Christians persistently praying for revival. And no awakening has continued long beyond the duration of such prayer.

These are historical facts. They should give pause to any Christian sincerely burdened for world revival.

Have you united with like-minded Christians in agonizing, consistent prayer for revival? Until you do, it is not likely you will see the results you thirst for in your own life, your church, your community — in the world.

You may say, "I have taken part in prayer meetings, from time to time, yet I have never witnessed any great outpouring of power."

This may be true.

I am convinced that the purpose of united prayer has often been frustrated because of a number of malpractices — intentioned or unintentioned — in prayer meetings.

In my experience as an evangelist throughout the world I have observed a great deal of ignorance and confusion on the matter of how to conduct a prayer meeting.

How long should one pray? How much planning should go into a prayer meeting? Should prayers be entirely spontaneous or should they be directed to specific subjects and needs? Should everyone kneel? Is the prayer meeting a time for personal confession of sins? Should audible expressions by other persons when one individual is praying be discouraged or encouraged?

It is not limiting the Holy Spirit to ask such questions. It is necessary to consider them, that all may be done "decently and in order."

Let us go into these questions one by one.

How long should one pray?

The place for long prayers is the "secret place," not in the congregation in worship. Some people are reluctant to pray in public because they feel that they could never achieve the lengthy petitions so often uttered by "professional" intercessors. It is far better to encourage people to pray for one subject at a time, in a sentence or a short paragraph, joining in prayer again after others have taken part.

Sir Wilfred Grenfell of Labrador was interested by (and interest afterwards led to conversion) D. L. Moody's remark in Edinburgh: "Let us sing Hymn No. 20 while our brother is finishing his prayer."

One of the things which drew me to Brazil in 1952 was the report that 81 churches in Sao Paulo had begun weekly prayer meetings for revival. I found that as many as 200 people were gathering for an hour's intercession in each church. Yet, unfortunately, the purpose of the meeting was being frustrated by various people monopolizing the time with long prayers.

In an effort to remedy this, I told them this story:

There was a movement of the Spirit in the city of Belfast, Ireland, when I was there in the 1930's. In a congregation of less than 200 there were between a dozen and a score of striking conversions every night.

When I asked the Presbyterian minister concerned to account for it, he replied, "Meet me at five o'clock in the morning and I'll show you."

I met him at the appointed hour and at ten minutes before

six we were in front of the church. We found 50 people
waiting outside for the church officer to let them in — to pray.

The people prayed in a simple way, in their own dialect.
A woman prayed for her wayward son in bad company, and
her prayer produced heart-felt "Amen's."

A working man prayed, "Lord, bless that poor woman
down our street, the one with the black eye. Lord, I'll try to
bring her and her drunken husband to the meeting tonight.
May the Holy Spirit bring them conviction and conversion,
Lord."

How Long to Pray?

A second-year theological student was in the meeting, and
these brief and homely prayers ill-suited his ideas of homilec-
tics. He decided to show the folks how to pray, and soon
was launched upon an oration with introduction, excellent
paragraphing and a theme running throughout the prayer.

"We thank Thee, Heavenly Father, that in spite of the
disobedience of our first parents, the seed of the woman
didst bruise the serpent's head, and Thy plan didst triumph.
We thank Thee, that, in spite of the wickedness of the
antedeluvian world, Thou didst shut the family of Noah in
the ark to preserve the seed, and Thy plan didst triumph.
We thank Thee that Abraham went out, not knowing
whither he went, and Thy plan didst triumph . . . "

He went on praying for 20 minutes. The minister whis-
pered to me, "This is terrible. When a man prays for three
minutes, you pray with him. When he prays for another
three minutes, you pray for him. And when he prays for
another three minutes, you're praying against him."

The theological student prayed on about Abraham and
Isaac and Jacob and the Children of Israel and Moses. He
was traveling with great velocity through the Second Book
of Kings when the minister interrupted him.

"Open your eyes, man," he said. "You're not praying. You're preaching a sermon."

The prayer stopped, and we returned to profitable intercession and sincere petition and we saw the answers come.

The humor of the story was used to guide the Brazilian Christians into proper paths of confession and petition and intercession. Those wonderful six o'clock-in-the-morning prayer meetings of the *Reavivamento Espiritual Brasilerio* (the Brazilian Spiritual Revival Movement) were used of God in every state of that vast country. Since then, the evangelical constituency of Brazil has increased from two million to more than five million in five years.

Should prayer meetings be planned? Or should prayer be entirely spontaneous?

Every measure should be taken to aid everyone present to "pray with the understanding," as Scripture enjoins us.

Everyone in the meeting should be able to hear every word uttered in prayer. Where there is a circle of intercessors kneeling, it is wise to invite the people to kneel facing each other and to raise their heads when raising their voices.

WHAT TO DO IN A LARGE PRAYER MEETING

When the meeting is too large for this, slips of paper bearing prayer requests should be passed to the chairman. These could be read and then the intercessors so led should rise and pray. Individual intercessors should be invited to stand and face the majority of the audience — and pray as loudly as desirable.

In one of the prayer meetings in which I participated in Brazil, after a united period of praise and exhortation, the people were directed to smaller rooms in groups of a dozen to a score, led by an experienced intercessor.

I have heard in some parts of the world in times of revival a dozen people or even a whole congregation praying aloud simultaneously. Sometimes this is of the Spirit. But it is not desirable to insist upon such praying. When simultaneous praying is artificially stimulated, the individual prayers may easily become mere ejaculations or repetitions, and are barriers to praying with understanding.

What is the proper posture in praying?

Some people feel that they must kneel to pray. That is ideal in private prayer. Some people may find they can abandon themselves more completely to prayer by praying prostrate — or by walking around while praying. This is an individual matter. Any posture is proper if it results in greater concentration and freedom in communing with the Spirit.

In a general prayer meeting, however, I think it best that each intercessor stand in his place so that everyone else has a good opportunity of hearing.

Are "amens" and other audible expressions desirable during public prayer?

Some groups desire informality in prayer while others insist upon dignity. Some are committed to liturgy while others to extemporaneity. In a united prayer meeting the feelings of each type of person should be respected.

Often, when the Spirit is moving, even quiet-minded people are stirred to "amens" and "hallelujahs." However, such expressions must not become mere ejaculations.

A minister in San Francisco was once praying: "Lord, we thank Thee for the resurrection of Jesus Christ. Someone has said, Lord, that the body of Jesus is still mouldering in a Syrian tomb . . ."

A chorus of amens from the unthinking brethren interrupted his thoughts.

Shocked, the minister went on, "Lord, I was referring to Robert Ingersoll."

There was a chorus of "God bless him."

In such a way can Satan turn what should be expressions of the soul into meaningless and even blasphemous utterances which grieve the Holy Spirit.

SHOULD SIN BE CONFESSED?

The ideal united prayer meeting should be a balanced combination of directed and undirected expression. The leader may suggest prayers for certain subjects and allow time for intercession concerning them. Or he may punctuate periods of prayer with a word of Scripture or a fitting hymn or a prayer from the Book of Common Prayer.

Is a united prayer gathering the place for personal confession of sin?

I believe that many potential revival movements have been diverted or dissipated by the public confession of matters best divulged in private. Throughout the Brazilian movement of 1952 there was not, to my knowledge, a single scandalous confession in public. Why? Because the people were instructed in Scriptural teachings regarding confession of sin, including its limitations. "Let the circle of the sin be the circle of the confession." This meant that secret sin required secret confession; private sin, private confession; open sin, open confession.

If confession of sin is made, it must be specific. "He shall confess that he has sinned in that thing . . ." (Leviticus 5:5). Confession of sin must be responsible. "Make confession to Him, and tell me now what thou hast done" (Joshua 7:19). Confession of sin must be thorough. "He that covereth his sins shall not prosper, but whoso confesseth and forsaketh them, shall have mercy" (Proverbs 28:13).

Following these suggestions will, I believe, open the way to real power in united prayer. Yet, rules, or forms cannot guarantee the efficaciousness of united prayer. As in private prayer, answers to prayer — the visible and experienced results of God's mighty power in the affairs of men — will come only when individuals are wholly surrendered to the will of God, allowing the Holy Spirit to indwell them. Anything less than this is bound to bring disappointment.

We know beyond doubt that the Spirit of God can use united prayer in a mighty way.

Exactly one hundred years ago began what is thought to have been the most effective revival in history. It began in New York City when a young man named Jeremiah Lanphier invited others to join him in a noon-day prayer meeting. From a gathering of six men grew a daily prayer movement involving thousands across the country. In early 1858, the movement was so potent that ten thousand converts were being added weekly to the New York churches. The movement spread throughout the world, adding millions to the churches, and quickening or converting such men as Moody and Alexander Whyte, Hudson Taylor and William Booth, Andrew Murray and Spurgeon. The effects of the work of grace were felt for fifty years.

Can such a revival occur today? I believe that it can. When Spirit-filled men and women unite in Spirit-directed prayers for revival, their persevering, persistent prayers will result in a mighty outpouring of God's Spirit such as the world has yet to see.

4. OVERCOME HINDRANCES TO PRAYER

Principal, Salvation Army School for Officers' Training, Chicago

The greatest prayer warriors have experienced it. You are praying in faith, in power, with effectiveness. Then something goes wrong. It is as though a telephone line during a conversation with a loved one has suddenly gone dead.

With Job, you cry in frustration and anguish, "Behold, I go forward, but he is not there; and backward, but I cannot perceive him. . . He hideth himself. . . I cannot see him" (Job 23:8, 9).

What are the causes of such times of aridity? God, who is eternally faithful, has given us definite assurances about prayer. "He shall call upon me, and I will answer him; I will be with him in trouble; I will deliver him and honor him" (Psalm 91:15). Christ assures us, "Ask, and it shall be given you; seek and ye shall find; knock, and it shall be opened unto you" (Luke 11:9).

Why then, should petitions ever end in disappointment and outstretched hands clasp only empty air?

Before going into the reasons, let me caution you that you cannot expect easy answers to all spiritual problems. Greater knowledge will come to you through the revelation of the Holy Spirit, through God's Word and prayer. But there will still be mysteries you cannot solve, depths you cannot plumb, heights you cannot reach as long as you remain earthbound. You will get some answers, but never enough to make trustful reliance unnecessary.

27

First, there are two reasons for a loss of power in prayer that stem from God. You must accept them in faith.

WHY GOD ALLOWS DISAPPOINTMENT

God may allow a temporary experience of disappointment and frustration as a test of your faith or integrity. This was so in the case of Job. He couldn't find God —.but God knew where Job was! Later Job could say, "But He knoweth the way that I take; when He hath tried me, I shall come forth as gold."

So, often, must we trust when the prayer line has seemed to go dead, knowing that divine silence does not mean divine absence.

Furthermore, every Bible-instructed Christian also knows that all prayers are not answered in the way we desire. Paul had experience with unanswered prayer (II Corinthians 12:7-9). He prayed for release from "a thorn in the flesh." Paul's specific request was not granted. But the answer he received was better than he asked for.

So, in our prayer, if nothing appears to happen, by seeking God's will and by expressing a true willingness to do His will, a quiet but steady spiritual growth will occur.

Your prayer, then, may seemingly lack power because God is testing you or is using the experience as a means of Christian discipline or growth. Having said this, however, I am firmly convinced that most unexpected and seemingly inexplicable times of powerlessness in the prayer life of sincere Christians result from barriers and hindrances within the believer.

Such hindrances can be rooted out. They can be overcome so that the channel to God is once more clear.

What are these hindrances?

1. Lop-sided praying — stressing petitionary prayer but neglecting worship, adoration, praise and thanksgiving — is

a common barrier in prayer. In other words, *using prayer only as a means of getting things.*

How easy it is to do this. We may even be unselfish in our everlasting petitions. We see so many needs — in our own lives, in the lives of our loved ones, in our church. We long to see God's supernatural power at work. And so our prayers are long cries of "Help, send, give, bless . . ."

This is immature, childish prayer.

We want to change things. God wants to change us.

Is Our Prayer Childish?

When we were children, parents had to do everything for us. But as we grew, father and mother did less and less for us, expecting us to grow up beyond the coddling, give-me, do-for-me era of childhood. Conversation is no longer limited to requests for things. It progresses to the language and the understandings of friendship and affection, of shared aspirations and stimulating companionships.

A friend of ours was dressing her four-year-old son one morning. In the process of adjusting an article of his clothing she had him standing first on one foot and then on the other. The little boy threw his arms around his mother's neck. This stirred her deeply and she said, "You do love your mummy, don't you?" And he replied with childish irritation, "No, I don't. I'm just holding on."

Some of us have not gotten beyond the "just holding on" reasons for prayer.

When we pray merely to get things, prayer becomes a matter of our personal convenience. We are likely to pray only when we want something. *It is therefore spasmodic, irregular, even infrequent.* Spiritual sensitivity and responsiveness are necessary to a sense of God's presence. These are inherent qualities of the life of the Spirit, not moods assumed, as a garment is put on, for an occasion. They are developed by long and diligent effort, by patient, devoted waiting upon God.

We cannot expect heart-warming fellowship if we rush in and rush out of God's presence. In the words of Brother Lawrence, "That practice which is alike the most holy, the most general, and the most needful in the spiritual life is the practice of the Presence of God. It is the schooling of the soul to find its joy in His Divine Companionship."

One of the prime objectives at the Salvation Army School for Officers' Training is to develop in our young officer-cadets a truly satisfying and effective prayer life. One hour each morning is given to prayer — a half-hour to a united prayer service and a half-hour to private devotions. At the beginning of each school year we find it necessary to counsel a number of our cadets concerning the proper use of their personal half hour. I remember one young man whose rejoinder was: "I don't need all that time. In fact I'm all 'prayed out' in five minutes."

We talked about using some time "getting tuned in" by use of the Word, reading a hymn or a suitable poem, then beginning prayer with thanksgiving, moving on to contemplation of God's goodness and holiness which almost inevitably leads to confession of our own failures and shortcomings. Prayer for today's responsibilities, opportunities and problems, for one's family, loved ones, for persons whom we know are having difficult battles, for the Kingdom at home and abroad, for our own church and its great objectives, for the peace of the world, for easing of racial tensions, for the salvation of the lost, for our own share in the work of the Kingdom — these and other petitions, not in a few hurried words, but in real thoughtful expressions of concern and faith. And all of this followed by a silent, thoughtful "waiting upon God" in which we surrender our wills to His and listen with devout responsiveness to allow Him to speak to us.

We have seen many young people come to a new understanding of prayer's potential. There has followed not only a more satisfactory prayer life but remarkable spiritual development.

2. The great barrier to free, effective communion with God is, of course, *sin*.

Isaiah is expressing a truth as old as Eden and as new as today in these words: "But your iniquities have separated between you and your God, and your sins have hid his face from you, that he will not hear" (Isaiah 59:2).

THE GREATEST BARRIER TO POWER

Prayers go unanswered because sin comes between God and man as a screen interfering with communication and obstructing the saving purposes of God. "If I regard iniquity in my heart, the Lord will not hear me" (Psalm 66:18).

This does not mean that God will not hear the penitential plea of the repentant sinner. Isaiah makes this clear in the first chapter of his prophecy (verses 16-18) when he speaks for God to sinners and promises that sins that stain the life can be cleansed as white as snow. The believer who is seduced into unbelief and disobedience can find ready forgiveness and renewed fellowship through our Advocate, Jesus Christ the Righteous (I John 2:1, 2).

But sin that is hidden in the heart, the concealed, disguised evils of the flesh and the spirit, these will impose a barrier that can muffle the sounds of our prayers so that they will never reach the Throne of Grace. If God seems far away, if an impassable barrier blocks your petitions, search your life for the evil that may lurk in dark recesses of the mind, for questionable habits, for carelessness, for selfishness. Ask the Spirit of God to bring such to light. Renounce anything done or left undone which you know to be contrary to the will of God.

In Salvation Army meetings, seekers after God are encouraged to come publicly to the front of the auditorium to pray at the "penitent form" or the holiness table. I recall a young woman who came to pray, a Salvationist in Army uniform, who spent an unusually long time kneeling and praying in tears. But in spite of her seeking, she finally left unsatisfied.

Do We Fool Ourselves?

Knowing her personally, I spoke to her. Her burden was that she no longer found any joy or gratification in her prayer life. We talked about many possible reasons, all to no avail. She phoned me some days later to say that victory, renewed communion and joy were now hers. The previously unadmitted barrier was a financial matter involving some returned merchandise which had, after some sharp bargaining, been taken back by the department store. The matter was outwardly settled. But it was not settled inwardly. The supposedly vaunted cleverness in the market place was revealed as shameful trickery in the place of prayer. When it was settled with the store it was settled at the altar.

If you would know God intimately you must be willing to heed the call of II Corinthians 6:17 and "come out from among them, and be ye separate, saith the Lord, and touch not the unclean thing." Then the promise of a true family relationship is yours with all the benefits of unimpaired communion and unimpeded power.

3. Lovelessness, whatever its expression, will separate us from God. This, of course, is sin. But it is such a serious and often overlooked obstacle to prayer, that it merits separate consideration.

We cannot be wrong with man and right with God. Any dishonesty, vengefulness, arrogance or animosity, selfishness in any form, will rear impassable barriers between ourselves and Eternal Love.

The truth is this: every act and aspect of life, all duties, all privileges, all associations — with no exceptions — affect our facility and potency in the moment of prayer.

Peter expressed this in connection with some homely advice to husbands and wives. The apostle counseled the husbands to act with understanding and love, "that your prayers be not hindered" (I Peter 3:7). The treatment of one's wife, therefore, is related to one's efficacy in prayer.

Jesus told us that if we come to the altar "and there rememberest that thy brother hath ought against thee; leave there thy gift before the altar, and go thy way; first be reconciled to thy brother, and then come and offer thy gift" (Matthew 5:23, 24). When connections are broken between man and man they are also broken between man and God.

We have been talking about prayer's problems and hindrances. Pointing out these obstacles would be in vain if there were not a means of overcoming them. Thank God there is an effective, infallible solution. The answer is not a philosophy nor a proposition. It is a Person: God the Holy Spirit — His indwelling Presence and power.

Too many Christians live an experience that is midway between Easter and Pentecost. Jesus lives, and they witness with faith to that truth. But they have no more joy nor power than did the disciples. In a sense, they huddle behind locked doors. It takes a Pentecostal experience to release us from our fears and frustrations. The Holy Spirit has been given to illumine the Word (John 16:13), to empower us (Acts 1:8) and to help our intercession (Romans 8:26,27). Is He yours in fullness?

In his book, *When the Holy Ghost Is Come*, Commissioner Samuel Logan Brengle puts it this way: "Now, when the Holy Spirit comes there pours into the soul not only a tide of love and simple faith, but a flood of light as well, and prayer becomes not only earnest, but intelligent also. Such men talk with God as a friend with friend, and the Holy Spirit helps their infirmities; encourages them to urge their prayer in faith; teaches them to reason with God; enables them to come boldly in the name of Jesus, when oppressed with a sense of their own insignificance and unworthiness; and, when words fail them and they scarcely know how to voice their desires, He intercedes within them with unutterable groanings, according to the will of God."

Prayer is "the Christian's native air," the center and source of your strength and joy. The maintenance of this link with God is vital to spiritual life and power. If you are wholly committed to the Holy Spirit the obstacles we have been talking about — lop-sided prayer, sin and lovelessness — can be conquered by the Spirit. Then if you have powerless prayers, the reason for them shall be in the greater wisdom of God and not in any lack or fault in yourself. "Let us therefore come boldly unto the throne of grace, that we may obtain mercy, and find grace to help in time of need" (Hebrews 4:16).

5. PRAYING THE WAY CHRIST TEACHES

BY ARMIN R. GESSWEIN
Director, Revival Prayer Fellowship

There are four forms of praying in the New Testament. Every one of these forms is found in connection with the great revivals in the history of the Church. Jesus Christ is the author and finisher of all four.

These are:

I. Individual or *private* praying.
II. The praying of *two in agreement.*
III. The praying of 2 or 3 or more in *groups.*
IV. The praying of *larger companies* and gatherings.

The first is private, the rest more public. One must never separate these four. Any Christian who will sincerely enter into one phase will readily become a part of the rest. Turning this around, if a Christian says he does not care for prayer-meetings, would "rather pray alone," a close check-up usually reveals that such a person is not praying very much alone either!

Jesus Christ is never against Jesus! The same Jesus who planned that I pray alone has also planned that I pray together with others. And, if I love Him and love the one form, I will love the others also.

Take a closer look at these four ways a Christian should pray. I prefer to speak of "praying" rather than "prayers" because Jesus teaches us "to pray" rather than to "say prayers." Also because we only learn to pray by praying — that is, by *doing it.*

I. PRIVATE PRAYING

Jesus taught: "But when you pray, go into your most private room, and closing the door, pray to your Father Who is in secret; and your Father Who sees in secret will reward you in the open" (Matthew 6:6, *Amplified New Testament*).

This kind of "closet" or "private room" praying must be first. It was so with our blessed Lord Jesus Himself. Whatever He taught about praying He practiced. That is what gives His statements and promises about prayer a quality all their own: because *no one ever prayed like Jesus!*

Yet, the big point in all His new teachings, commands and promises about praying is just this: that *we are to learn not some kind of praying — we are to learn His own kind of praying, and receive His kind of answers!* This is new, thrilling, terrific!

He taught Matthew 6:6 the way He Himself was constantly practicing it. His "private room" was out in nature as a rule: on some mountain or hill, out in the desert or beneath some olive tree that was off the beaten path. It was as He was "alone praying" (doing it) that one of His disciples asked, "Lord, teach us to pray" (Luke 11:1).

A man once came to Gipsy Smith, the celebrated English evangelist, and asked him how to have revival.

Said Gipsy: "Do you have a place where you can pray?"

"Yes," was the reply.

"Tell you what to do," Gipsy said. "You go to that place, and take a piece of chalk along. Kneel down there. And with the chalk draw a complete circle all around you — and pray for God to send revival on everything inside of the circle!"

Then he added, "Stay there until He answers — and you will have revival!"

I think that was one of the clearest answers ever given

to the question people are asking from time to time — "How does a revival begin?"

My observation, from Scripture and from experience, is that it usually begins with *one* praying Christian, and that one need not be a preacher. Any one will do, for Jesus promises, *"Every one that asketh receiveth"* (Luke 11:10). If the times got so bad that only one intercessor was left on earth, like Elijah, we could still have revival. This is a tremendous word for times of declension and apostasy: "The effectual fervent prayer of a righteous man availeth much" (James 5:16b).

Now, about *time* and *place*. *When* shall we pray? and *where?*

"What if I don't have a 'private room'?" someone might ask.

In reply I would say this: If Jesus told you to go into your "most private room," you must have one somewhere. Ask Him to show you where it is. It could be that you have not found it yet, or have not asked Him to point it out to you.

This leads me to say that *the thing of first importance in prayer is to have a place where you can pray.* Many fail right here. They never get into the wonderful holy habit of daily praying simply because they do not have a place to pray. We read that Jesus "continued His habit of retiring to lonely spots and praying" (Luke 5:16, Williams).

In one of Norway's revivals a young girl was wonderfully converted to Christ. But she said she had no place to pray, for she was the only Christian in a family of many children. She could not find a place at home in which to get quiet and alone.

Quoting Matthew 6:6, I told her that Jesus must have a place for her somewhere, a "closet" where she could "pray in secret," for He said distinctly, "enter into *thy* closet." I suggested that she ask Him where it was.

The next time I saw her she said with beaming face that she had found it. She said the Lord showed her that she should go over to the church during her noon hour. It was just across from her school. There, right in the sanctuary of God, she found her place and firmly formed the daily habit of private prayer, and she began to be rewarded openly with many answers.

My wife testifies that she used to go up into a room on the third story of her home in the north of Norway, to pray every day. One of her prayers was that God would grant her His choice of a life-partner. God answered by sending the writer of these lines all the way from America! God gave us both His answer, for He had given us each a "private room" in which to pray.

II TWO PRAYING IN AGREEMENT

Jesus taught: "Again I tell you, that if two of you agree (harmonize together, together make a symphony) about — anything and everything — whatever they shall ask, it will come to pass and be done for them by My Father in heaven" (Matthew 18-19, *Amplified New Testament*).

Anything and everything. We might say that the sky is the limit! This is without doubt one of the most powerful promises in the Word of God. The point, however, is not only in two people praying together, but in their complete agreement (symphony). This is the difficulty, and only the Lord can bring two together like that. When the full story is told, this is invariably found to be part of the pattern of revival praying.

Charles G. Finney, the mighty revivalist, found many of the Lord's best secrets. But this was one of His simplest and deepest secrets. When he came to a new community for revival services, usually in the first meeting he would ask: "Has anyone heard from heaven? Is anyone hearing from God about these meetings?" If, out of a large audience he found even one such faithful intercessor — one who had a burden from God and who had assurance of being heard — he would "agree" with that person before God and continue before Him in such agreement in prayer, and *would practically announce that God would give a revival in that place!* He would take on tremendous boldness and confidence at the mere finding of one such Christian in that area.

In keeping with this promise of two, Finney usually had a man of great prayer and intercession traveling with him, such as Abel Clary at one period and "Father" Nash, as he was called, at another. Nash often did not even appear in the public meetings, but gave himself almost continually to prayer during the services. Finney preached backed by this secret prayer agreement. He seldom failed to witness strong revival in the wake of his preaching.

This agreement of two is most versatile and suggests many patterns. Our Lord surely had husband and wife in mind when He spoke of it. In other generations many Christian parents found in it a new secret of strength, especially when praying for their children.

A godly old pastor of Oslo, Norway, used to say that if Christian parents were truly one in Christ and in this kind of agreement in their prayers for children, they would not go wrong — their children would be saved. He had observed this through his many years (he was then 80). His own three children were not only converted, but were blessed and used of the Lord. He said also that if the children did not turn to the Lord, it was his observation that somewhere the parents were not in full oneness in their praying before the Lord. This promise to two praying in agreement should be a great challenge and tremendous encouragement to Christian parents.

III. THE PRAYING OF SMALLER GROUPS

Jesus taught: "For wherever two or three are gathered (drawn together as My followers) in (into) My name, there am I in the midst of them" (Matthew 18:20, *Amplified New Testament*).

In prayer Jesus covers the whole range of man — individual and social. Revival is both individual and corporate. God revives the individual, but never just by his lonesome! Revival usually starts with one praying Christian and then moves on to others who are like-minded. We might say that it moves on in that same original oneness: from one to others, but keeping to oneness, keeping all in spiritual oneness with that one.

I would rather use the words *one* and *oneness* than unity, because in John 17 Jesus prayed "that they all may be *one*." In that prayer He declares further that two massive results would follow: a) the world would believe and b) the world would *know* that God had sent Him.

We must stress this: *in all true prayer, no matter how large or small the groups, this loving oneness of heart ("one accord") is important.* This is the heart of all revival. It often is found in a remnant in a community, or even in a church. But not a clique! Revival-glory is manifested at this kind of altar-fellowship. God's holy Shekinah is always first revealed to those who are thus united in prayer in the innermost part of His holy temple.

The smaller groups are everywhere. They represent the revival-remnant in the land. They are the harbingers of every true revival. They are often called cells or fellowship groups. They remind us of the great Methodist awakening which was carried forward by the many "class meetings" — the heart of Methodism.

In a sense the most significant trend of our times is the fresh emergence of many kinds of prayer groups and prayer fellowships, both in the churches and inter-church. In Billy Graham's New York Crusade, Tom Allan of Scotland told many ministers' groups of such "koinonia" (fellowship) groups in his parish, and in other parts. He testified to the quickening of more than one entire congregation through such group formations.

Colleen Townsend Evans, in an article, "Prayer Cells Changed My Life" (Feb. '54 *Youth for Christ Magazine*) writes: "Since 1947 when my husband, Louis, and I had a 'right about face' experience in our lives, we have been a part of one or more prayer cells. Through the years they have been the keys to a deeper life with Christ . . .

"I remember well my first experience in corporate prayer. I was a spanking new Christian and had been invited to join a prayer cell of powerful, 'old soldier' Christians. Prayer for them was work, real business and contact with the living God! I had never known anything like that.

"It took many weeks before I could forget the person next to me, to stop thinking how my inexperienced prayers would sound to the others, and mainly just to forget myself and pray from my heart. I read my first prayer and was scared stiff. But soon, through private prayer and practice, I found that God was not the people about me, but that I was praying to Him and not to them. I began to look forward to the prayer cell, instead of being relieved when it was over. I found a new release in my Christian life.

"I thought I had close friends before, and I did, but nothing compared to the friendships now developed through praying together. Something happens in those hours when you meet together on your knees before God, bonds not produced by the most gracious of social times. Christ says, 'By this shall all men know that ye are my disciples, if ye have love one for another.' (John 13:35) . . . **The prayer cell produces it, and the world notices it.**"

IV. FULL PRAYER-MEETING PRAYING

Jesus commands it: "And being assembled together with them, (He) *commanded* them . . . (to) wait for the promise of the Father" (Acts 1:4) . . . "These *all* continued with one accord in prayer and supplication, with the women, and Mary the mother of Jesus, and with his brethren" (Acts 1:14).

Here Jesus brings prayer up to its highest capacity — *total congregation praying.* When praying reaches this strength, we know we are on the eve of great revival. Yes, we are already in it.

In the Upper Room in Jerusalem (the first church) Jesus had for the first time in history gotten together about 120 members of the church — every one of them a strong intercessor. A literal rendering is that they "persisted obstinately" in prayer. There was great supplication. 120 intercessors all together praying — that is an all-time high in the record of Scripture to this point.

Indeed, this was not only a miracle, but the highest and last great miracle of the Risen Christ on earth, before He went to heaven!

And, to this hour, a great all-out prayer meeting in any congregation is still the highest miracle of Christ in any community! What is there on earth to compare with it? It is rare indeed, and the devil fights it.

Dr. A. T. Pierson used to say that there never was a revival in history but by united supplicatory praying, and he added that no revival ever continued beyond the continuation of the same. This is Christ's amazing pattern for the pathway to revival. How can we hope to see a revival in this generation when the prayer-meetings are so low and veak and puny?

We have forgotten that when Christ built His church, He built a prayer meeting!

We have forgotten that there was not a single member of that Jerusalem congregation who was not in the prayer meeting!

We have forgotten that it advanced on its knees, all through the 28 chapters of the book of Acts.

We have forgotten that the place where they counted their numbers was in the prayer meeting.

We have forgotten that united prayer was its supreme method for everything — that everything was done by prayer. We have forgotten that prayer was the very organizing principle of that church: of its new oneness and unity of its officers, of its victory in battle against every form of persecution and opposition.

United praying was its method of promoting and propagating the Gospel, until the banner of the cross was unfurled in the very palaces of the Caesars!

When Satan tried to stop the advance of that praying church, he did not bother to try to break up their power, or their unity — all he had to do was to break up their praying. That is just where he could *not* get them. But that seems to be the place where he has gotten us today.

All the way through, the book of Acts shows the intimate and unfailing connection between prayer and every work of God. If God would do apart from prayer what He has promised to do in answer to prayer, then the very point of prayer would break down.

When God is about to do a work on the earth, He always starts by waking up His people and calling them back to prayer. When prayer is on the increase — all these four forms of prayer — then we know that revival is at the door.

6. CONVERSATIONAL PRAYER

BY ROSALIND RINKER
Christian Counselor and Author

I stumbled upon the conversational prayer approach to God as a young missionary in Peiping, China. The traditional "you-take-your-turn-and-pray-until-you're-finished" and then "I'll-take-my-turn-and-pray-until-I'm-finished" method left me vaguely dissatisfied. As a rule I was relieved when group prayer meetings were over.

Then one day a new door opened.

My friend Mildred Rice and I were praying for two of our students, Ming-lee and her sister-in-law. Suddenly I remembered that Ming-lee had sent a note to me that morning saying the situation for which Mildred was praying had already cleared up.

Without stopping to think, I interrupted her prayer and continued it as mine: "Thank You, Lord. You have already answered that prayer. Ming-lee has already been able to forgive her sister-in-law."

Startled by my own audacity at interrupting Mildred's prayer, I stopped. There was a moment of silence, and then with great relief both of us sat back on our heels and laughed.

"Well, isn't that something!" said Mildred. Meaning both the early answer to prayer *and* the natural spontaneous way in which the news about Ming-lee had popped out. We settled down on our knees to pray again, with a warm sense of His nearness.

It was a natural experience. I knew the Lord was trying

to break through our hide-bound tradition to teach us something important. We wondered if we should pray shorter prayers and give the Holy Spirit more opportunity to guide us as we prayed.

Mildred and I talked it over. Instead of making solo prayer-speeches, as it were, we would include Him, as a Third Party, and talk things over with Him, waiting for Him to speak to us, to guide us, to help us know what to pray.

Mildred thought of another angle. "We could bring up one person or one situation at a time. Then we could both pray back and forth about it, until we feel we have touched God and our hearts are at rest."

Quietly, reverently, and with our attention focused on the Lord Jesus there with us, we began to converse with Him. All the "padding" of unnecessary and acquired prayer language slipped away. There seemed to be no need of the finality of an "amen" at the close of each short sentence prayer, for we were conversing with God. I spoke, she spoke, and we waited for Him to speak in that still, small voice within our hearts. Prayer took on a new freshness. With courage we began to ask for "mountains to be moved."

Soon we were helping our newly converted Chinese friends to pray conversationally and were astonished at the rapid spiritual growth they made. It wasn't long before our regular mission prayer meetings were being transformed by this same freshness.

'I' REPLACES 'WE'

We found many other practical things which began to delight us. There was honesty. To say "I" when we meant I, and not to hide behind the familiar editorial "we" was sometimes a painful, purging kind of honesty. There was no shifting of prayer responsibility by giving "requests," an unconscious device often used as a cover-up for our own unfaced sins or failures. Each one brought his own requests to the Lord and then as we were led by the Spirit, we prayed for one another right on the spot. This brought the supernatural harvest of love, and how we began to love one another!

Conversational prayer is no innovation. Since my discovery of it I've found many groups of young people using this direct, honest approach to God.

Conversational prayer is simply a conversation between those who love one another. The Lord Jesus Christ Himself urged us to converse together with each other and with Him:

"Again I say unto you, that if two of you shall agree on earth as touching any thing that they shall ask, it shall be done for them of my Father which is in heaven. For where two or three are gathered together in my name, there am I in the midst of them" (Matthew 18:19, 20).

Conversational prayer is talking as we ordinarily would do in a group — each person taking many turns, praying by subjects in a natural way that holds everyone's attention because everyone is taking part. And all the while being conscious that the Lord is present.

Learn In Twenty Minutes

Here is the true story of how a group of young people learned to pray conversationally in about twenty minutes.

Several years ago Ray Williamson, student leader of the Inter-Varsity group at Santa Barbara State College, invited me to attend one of the quarter hour noon prayer meetings. As we walked across the campus I asked him if there was any special way in which the meeting was conducted.

"Yes, there is," replied Ray. "I usually start, and then the person next to me prays, and we go on around the circle until everyone has prayed."

"Ray, how does that give the Holy Spirit an opportunity to lead you while you pray?" I asked.

"What do you mean, Ros?"

I tried to explain. "Well, you see, it's like this: The Holy Spirit within us moves our hearts, initiates our concerns, our love and our requests. Could it be possible that in 'going around the circle' humanly speaking you might quench the Spirit?"

"Quench the Spirit?"

"Yes, by following a set pattern. That makes it difficult for the Spirit to move us as we pray, and to make us aware of what He is saying. Didn't you ever have a wonderful prayer idea while the other fellow was praying, and say to yourself, 'Now I must be sure to remember what it was'?"

Ray laughed. "I'm beginning to see what you're driving at, Ros, and it makes sense. Why don't you tell us about it, and show us how. Right now."

Knowing the fifteen minutes would go by quickly, I spoke briefly to the group gathered under a big tree.

"Instead of going around the circle today, let's remember the Lord Jesus is right here, in the center of this circle. He promised, 'Where two or three are gathered, there am I.' Let's speak directly to Him, simply, honestly, just like we talk to a person in whom we have real confidence. Let's say 'I' when we mean I, and 'we' when we mean the whole group.

ONE SUBJECT AT A TIME

"Another important thing is to pray by subjects. If someone starts to pray for Joe Blow, two or three of the rest of you feel perfectly free to pray for him too. Be direct and simple. Then let's be quiet a moment before introducing a new name. The Spirit will guide us. You can each pray four or five times if you want to, but let's keep to one subject at a time. And let's remember to make our prayers very short, and to pray back and forth."

After a moment of silence, I prayed first. "Lord Jesus, thank You for being here. You said You would be, and we all thank You together, and worship you. (Pause) Guide us now, as to whom we should pray for first."

Ray took it up. "Lord, I want to pray for Tony, that Italian boy in my swim class. He's my buddy, and I've been wanting to talk to him about You, but I haven't done it yet. Please help me."

A young man across the circle took it next: "Why, Lord, I hadn't any idea Ray was in Tony's swim class. I've already talked to him about You. Bless Ray and give him faith and courage and love for Tony. And help us to work together now."

A girl in the circle gasped audibly, "Oh, how wonderful!" Her spontaneous prayer continued, "Lord, I sit right next to Tony in an English lit class, and I've already lent him a Christian magazine. I was just wishing Tony knew some Christian guy who'd talk to him. Why, isn't this wonderful! I had no idea that both Ray and Ted knew Tony!"

Several members of the group prayed for these three and their further contacts with Tony, and for Tony that his heart might be open to receive Christ.

I prayed again, "Lord, guide Ted and Ray definitely. Show them the next step. Show them what you want them to do tomorrow. Help them show Your love to Tony in some definite way."

Later, Ray asked, "Ros, tell us more. Why, we were praying back there! What else can you tell us? Is there any more?"

There is always more. One of the most exciting discoveries some of us made while working with these students was what we call *faith-sized requests*. That is, in a particular situation, to pray for some specific person or thing, and to ask only for what we really believe God can do in a given time limit.

The Rev. Harold De Vries, pastor of the Winnetka (Ill.) Bible Church, heard about conversational prayer and he decided he would try it out at the prayer meeting. He asked the Lord to send 150 persons to the next Wednesday night prayer meeting. Then he remembered — *faith-sized requests.* He asked himself if he really expected God could send 150 people.

After consideration he changed his prayer, "Lord, I believe you *can* and *will* send 100 interested persons to prayer meeting this Wednesday night."

There were 100 interested persons there that night. By the next Sunday another 50 had signed up. Now 150 people are meeting regularly in about 25 small groups of from two to six, in homes, in offices, in the suburbs and in the loop. The needs of the people are being met. There is spontaneous prayer for one another. Faith-sized requests are being answered. More people are taking part. There are fewer cliches, less padding and more honesty in prayer. Men and women are coming closer to God and to each other in the Winnetka Bible Church.

You Must Be Honest

This could happen in your church, or in your group. All God needs is a man or a woman who knows something of the vital power of honest prayer, and who has experienced the truth found in Matthew 18: 19, 20.

To carry on conversational prayer means to talk with God in a conversational manner. Conversation is an art some of us may have to cultivate.

In good conversation we are considerate of one another. There is a give and take of ideas, all contributing to a specific subject. And each person uses his memory to recall, his patience to wait, his alertness to jump in, his willingness to get out, and above all his capacity to hold back the disruptive. In other words, he is in tune.

These points can and do apply to conversational prayer. Through it, those who will discipline their minds and their audible prayers can find a new world of "togetherness" with the Lord and each other awaiting them.

7. YOUR PRAYER CAN SHAKE THE WORLD

BY CLIFFORD H. RICHMOND
Pastor, Chevy Chase (Md.) Methodist Church

In the San Fernando Valley are municipal wells sunk 100 to 500 feet deep into the earth. A clock-like apparatus reveals and measures the agitation of the water. What happens at the far end of the earth is felt in California. An earthquake which disturbs any region in the world causes the water level to rise.

Scientists tell us that if you drop a pin to the earth a tiny vibration is sent to every other part of the earth. In other words, the material universe is so much one that each and every bit of matter affects and may be affected by each and every other bit of matter.

This is true not only with respect to matter, but it is also true in the realm of energy. In 1934 when Admiral Byrd was at the South Pole he flashed a radio signal which caused a hammer to strike and ring the Liberty Bell in Independence Hall in Philadelphia, Pa. We are learning more and more about such non-physical rays and using them in radio, television, radar and x-ray. Of course we're all becoming familiar with the limitless possibilities of atomic energy released by the splitting of the atom.

What has all this got to do with prayer?

You've no doubt wondered, "How can my prayers affect others and the world in which I live?" Here is the answer. In our material universe and the realm of energy, what happens in one place tends to affect every other place. This is likewise true in respect to the spiritual energy we generate through prayer.

51

When a person prays, something happens which would not have happened if he had not prayed.

Something not only happens to the individual who prays, but to those for whom he prays and to the world through their prayers. Jesus, of course, knew it, taught it and practiced it.

In His high priestly prayer in the seventeenth chapter of the gospel of John, He says: "I pray for them. I pray not for the world, but for them which thou has given me . . . . I pray not that thou shouldest take them out of the world, but that thou shouldest keep them from the evil . . . . Neither pray I for these alone, but for them also which shall believe on me through their word."

The Scriptures indicate the main work of Jesus today — "He ever liveth to make intercession for them" (Hebrews 7:25).

If Christ attached so much importance to intercessory prayer, a solemn responsibility rests upon us as Christians to learn how to unleash this power in the world today.

How can we do it?

How to 'Broadcast' Prayer Power

First, the effectiveness of our prayer for others depends upon the depth of our own spiritual lives. Think of your radio or TV set. The more power your receiver has, the better is your reception. The same thing is true of a broadcasting station. The greater number of watts, the more effective the broadcasting.

So it is with us. The clearer the channel, the greater our trust and purity of life. The more conscious we are of God's presence and power, the more powerful our prayers are. Not until we are fully committed to the Holy Spirit, willing to let Him cleanse us and baptize us with power can He use us effectively in intercessory prayer.

A second requisite for effective prayer for others is intensity of thought and emotion. We must pray with sincerity, earnestness, overwhelming desire. The half-hearted never have much success in intercessory prayer.

John Knox prayed: "Give me Scotland or I die," and he held on to God until Scotland came under the saving and redeeming power of the Eternal One.

The little group of early Christians prayed for Peter who was in prison and they kept on praying until he was miraculously released and stood in their midst.

Third, Christ taught us to be persistent in our prayer. He told the story of the man who had guests late one night and went to his friend's house for bread. His friend was in bed and at first would not respond to his requests, but through persistent knocking and pleading the friend finally gave in and provided him with bread needed. Jesus also told of the widow who went to a judge seeking justice in a certain situation in her life. She kept coming to him until finally to get rid of her he granted her request.

Jesus didn't mean to say that God was like either of these men and had to be forced into doing things for His children.

The point He wanted to make was that if these men who were human would respond to persistency, how much more would our Heavenly Father — God Himself — hear and answer the persistent prayers of His children!

We are not trying to change God's mind or get Him to do something He doesn't want to do. We are simply giving Him the opportunity to do for us what He most desires to do.

There are certain blessings which can come only by much persistent prayer. There are some blessings which God gives to all, whether they are good or bad: sunshine and rain; seedtime and harvest. But there are other blessings He can give only to those who turn to Him. And the more sincerely and persistently we turn to Him the greater the blessings He can give.

A school teacher may try to teach all her pupils alike. But she finds she can do more for some than for others because they are more responsive. They are hungrier and thirstier for knowledge. The same thing is true in the home. Parents may love all their children equally as well and want to do as much for one as for the other. But they find they can do more for some of their children, get closer to some than to others, simply because these children are more cooperative and responsive.

GOD NEEDS COOPERATION

So God can do more for us if we are cooperative and responsive. He can release more of His blessings to those who come to Him in earnest, persistent prayer.

Starr Daily's father prayed earnestly for his boy's salvation for 25 years. But his boy appeared to be a confirmed criminal. He never lived to see his boy give up his life of crime. Shortly after his death, however, Jesus Christ appeared to Starr Daily in prison and touched his heart and made him a new creature. He became a great Christian author. His father's prayers were not in vain. A man less stalwart in prayer could never have won such a victory!

The disciples in the Upper Room prayed day and night for ten days until the Holy Spirit came upon them. If they had grown discouraged after a day or so of praying these men might never have experienced the power and glory of Pentecost.

There is a lot of sorrow, sin and sickness in the world today because we are not praying for others. The Lord is thwarted in His desire and willingness to heal, bless and save the people of our world simply because we are not praying. We are too half-hearted, too indifferent. We could bring the world to Christ and Christ to the world if we would only get down on our knees and do some wrestling with Almighty God.

Closing the Circuit

On January 21, 1930, the most far-reaching radio broadcast up to that time was scheduled. It was the message of King George at the opening of the session of the London Naval Arms Conference. The whole world for the first time was to be brought within the voice of the king. The United States, however, almost missed it. A few minutes before the king was to speak, a member of the control room staff of the Columbia Broadcasting System tripped over a wire and broke it, thus severing connections. Harold Vivian, chief control operator, immediately grasped the ends of the broken wires, one in each hand, and restored the circuit. The shock of 250 volts of electricity shook his arms and went through his body, but he held on until new wires were connected. The king's speech came to America through the tingling body of Harold Vivian.

The King of kings wants to broadcast to our world. He has many things to say, to do, to give to needy men. But the circuit has been broken. He has put you, as a Christian, in a position to close it, through intercessory prayer.

As you pray for others, with one hand you reach down to a needy, lost and suffering world and with the other reach up to the all-sufficient God and let His message of redemption, healing and blessing flow through you, so that everyone will come to know and love Him who is King of kings and Lord of lords!

8. HEALING PRAYER

BY SAMUEL M. SHOEMAKER

Rector, Calvary Episcopal Church, Pittsburgh, Pa.

You cannot read any of the four gospels without being struck with the amount of space given to some kind of healing.

"And Jesus went about in all Galilee, teaching in their synagogues, and preaching the good tidings of the kingdom, and healing all manner of disease and all manner of sickness among the people" (Matthew 4:23).

This verse is only the prelude to a record which is filled with stories of healing. You may say that this preponderance is because of the fact that people love wonders, and the miracles of healing are surprising. But whatever the motive in recording them, no one can doubt that Jesus spent much time caring for the ills of human beings and bringing to them new health.

The healing was not only of body. The word translated "disease" in this passage really means "weakness," or "softness" and the word translated "sickness" means sickness of body or of mind. It was the whole personality, therefore, with which Jesus was dealing, and the whole personality which was healed.

EXPECT MIRACLES TODAY?

If we had been in the company of Jesus, traveling with Him and watching Him work and absorbing His spirit of faith, there would probably have been a quiet expectation of such manifestations of power. Should we have this

56

expectation today? Yes! *Insofar as we are today in His company and in touch with His Spirit, we shall feel the same way.*

"Miracles" will not be any the less wonderful, but they will be a greater expression of something we already know, rather than a mystifying exhibition of something totally unfamiliar in our own experience.

It would be easy to think of miracles in what you might call a purely materialistic way. Here was a man with epilepsy, or a woman with a hemorrhage — it was a physical malady. Jesus came along with supernatural power, directed it against the illness and dissipated it.

TWO FACETS OF INFLUENCE

I am sure that this conception of miracles makes them harder to believe in, and does not really explain what happened. It leaves out two supremely important factors.

The first factor is the effect of Jesus' personality. I do not mean His engagingness, but *His manifest single-mindedness and spiritual clarity and faith.*

I am sure that Jesus wanted most of all to get these people into touch with God. Notice the order of our verse: "Jesus went about in all Galilee, teaching in their synagogues, and preaching the good tidings of the kingdom, and healing . . . ." When you came within the orbit of His influence, life took on a new dimension. There was power in Him, and that power flowed out of Him. It was supernatural, but it was such power as we can share in, for His own contemporaries did in some measure share in it. We might almost say that, important as it was, His healing of people was incidental. *The main thing is always our relationship to Him, and after that the blessings He may give.*

The second factor is the positive inner reaction of the person in need of healing. In other words — faith. Often we consider "faith" to be a developed intellectual attitude which we are not ready to acknowledge. I am sure faith is fundamentally much more like courage or loyalty or adventure than it is like reason or logic or philosophy. There is a difference between sitting on a bank and watching others swim, and flinging oneself into the stream and trying to learn by doing it. Analysis without experiment will produce very little faith.

Some people become so set and sodden in their long-accepted doubts that nothing can move them off their dead-center. They will even deny themselves a blessing like healing in order to preserve their intellectual skepticism. What they sometimes call "intellectual integrity" is often nothing but silly pride holding on to an old viewpoint while standing in the presence of obvious power that can help them, and denying what their eyes see.

Faith is a kind of willingness to cooperate. It sees power flowing into and through others. It calls out to that Power. God responds to those cries from the wilderness.

Now, what about ourselves and our own time?

True, there is some mystery about healing, for not all who seek, even in real faith, are healed. Paul prayed that his "thorn in the flesh" might be removed, but it was not removed. All he heard was, "My grace is sufficient for thee." That is why Christ, and faith in Him, must come first: we can always have the healing of finding Him, whether or not He grants the other healing which we may want. I am convinced, however, that a heaven of power lies round about us which most Christians never deeply touch, and that if we really seek and believe we will know a vastly greater measure of healing than most of us now enjoy. We will know more *health*, less *conflict*, less *fatigue*, less *strain*, more *peace*, more *energy*, more *joy*.

DOORWAY TO WHOLENESS
Now there is one door-way through which I think a great deal of healing may come: to the mind, to the body, the emotions, to the whole personality. That is through what is called the "sub-conscious," or "unconscious."

Modern psychology has made us aware of a hidden self, composed of memories and impressions that seem never to be forgotten. You know how in a dream a memory will rise that you may not have thought about for years. You know how a name you cannot remember when you try will sometimes "come back" to you if you let the matter rest for a little time. The abiding place of these bits of information is this area we call the "sub-conscious." Out of this region probably come many of the conflicts which destroy people, and the energies which make them great. A sub-conscious in good working order is a boon. But a sub-conscious full of fear or hate or negative thinking can make you sick and hostile and very unhappy.

It may help to think of the sub-conscious as a kind of cellar of the human personality. It can be musty and damp, dirty and in disorder, infested with rats. Or it can be a kind of engine-room where life energies are generated.

PRAYER, THE KEY
How can we clean up the cellars of the mind and emotions? We can have an indirect effect on the sub-conscious by the kind of thoughts we allow to stay in our conscious mind, for these seem to trickle through into the sub-conscious. But there is a more direct approach to the sub-conscious. It is through *prayer*.

Our own prayers can make a great deal of difference. As we pray, it appears that the power of God can use our seeking as entrance into the conscious and unconscious mind. You have often known a stillness and power to steal over you where you have been agitated and afraid.

But still more, I think, do the *prayers of others* have power in our sub-conscious lives. Apparently the love that another feels for us in our need is greater in its spiritual potency than any concern we can feel for ourselves. The prayer of another may be less contaminated by anything that can be selfish. The more love and faith one has, and the more he will center his praying directly upon the sub-conscious of the other person, the more frequent seem to be the answers. The famous literacy missionary, Dr. Frank C. Laubach has told me that sometimes he will stand alone in an empty room, turn in the direction where a person is for whom he is praying, call his name three times, and then ask God for the blessing he wants for him. Through such praying we seem to become one step in God's whole merciful, creative will for people; we help to release His love and His power.

Let me give you an illustration.

A man came to see me. He had once tried suicide, and a friend had "happened" to come to his house, found him in the garage with the exhaust pouring into the car from a hose attached to it, drew him out and took him to the hospital. This man had also fought alcohol for years, and after a long victory had recently slipped again. Discouraged, he went to a library near his home and took down a little book of mine called *How You Can Find Happiness*. He read it three times, and decided he must see the person who wrote it.

He called to make an appointment at once. My secretary said my time was filled up all day, but he said, "I am coming anyway" and rang off.

That evening I happened to come home 15 minutes early for dinner. This man was waiting for me.

We sat down, and he talked for about five minutes. His frame was tense, his eyes red. As he talked, I prayed.

When he stopped talking, I said something like this: "I believe you are carrying around in your subconscious feelings that you are not only guilty but incorrigible."

"Yes," he said, "I am."

I said, "May I pray directly for your subconscious — even pray 'at' it?"

"Yes," he said.

For a few moments we prayed with concentration. To my concern and faith, and his need and hope, God added the power of His Holy Spirit.

When I stopped, he looked up and said, "It is amazing what can happen in so short a time. Those thoughts about suicide are absolutely gone."

MIRACLE BEGUN

We met next day, and a quiet, smiling gentleman told me again of the beginnings of the miracle in his life.

I believe that anyone with love and faith and prayer could have brought that experience to him.

So many people today need that kind of caring and attention, the atmosphere of Christian love and faith, the experiment of prayer directed right at the point of need! How many would keep out of hospitals and psychiatric wards! How many of us in the church need to let Christ heal our emotions; transform the content of our subconscious!

There is a conversion that does not extend to the subconscious, and then there is a conversion that *does* extend to the sub-conscious. When a man's whole self is attuned to Christ, you have not only great integration and joy, but also great capacity and power..

Let us pray to the Lord Jesus Christ to heal us all the way through, and send us out whole into a sick world with His holiness and His wholeness!

9. THE UPSIDE-DOWNNESS OF PRAYER

BY NORMAN P. GRUBB

General Secretary, Worldwide Evangelization Crusade

Most of us have a basic misconception of the character of prayer. We regard it as the human upreach of the soul to God. Actually, it is the divine downreach of God to the soul.

This definition of prayer is not just a play on words, an attempt to talk about prayer in a different way. Apprehension of the reality of what I am saying can bring a vital difference to your life, put new meaning into prayer.

RELATIONSHIP DEFINED

How? First, let me clarify the relationship between the divine and the human.

What we call the Christian life — in reality just life itself or eternal life — only starts when the human personality has become the container of the divine — *of God Himself*. The human self was never created for any other purpose than to manifest the divine Self.

Now, a human being without God as the real Self within it is sub-human. He is in the condition that the Bible calls dead ("dead while she [or he] liveth," as Paul described it in I Timothy). He has a false self-centered existence derived from Satan, the spirit of self-centeredness who has possessed all men since the fall of Adam.

When a person comes to Christ, however, redemption severs the bond between the satanic spirit and the human spirit at the cross of Christ. This bond is replaced by a new union in the resurrection — the union between the liberated human spirit and the Holy Spirit. Man in Christ has become God-indwelt, has been restored by grace to the status of normal humanity: "I will dwell in them and walk in them"; "It is God that worketh in us to will and to do of His good pleasure"; "I live, yet not I, but Christ liveth in me." The Bible says it in a thousand ways.

Here, now, we have the groundwork for an understanding of prayer.

God, the Compassionate, the world Saviour, the Self-Giver, never ceases to express Himself through His body. That is, through you and me. He sees, thinks, feels through us.

SOURCE OF PRAYER

Prayer, therefore, is an indication that *God is stirring within us concerning some special need.*

This is why the solution to dryness or deadness in the prayer life is not to "try" to pray more, but *to give up praying.* In place of the prayer of self-effort, relax back into the recognition of the Indwelling Person. See Him, flow along with Him in thankfulness, praise, love (for these also are the movings of His Spirit in us, in literal fact God praising God, God loving God). As we do this, we shall soon find that He is sharing His outlook and concern with us, looking through *our* eyes; and we shall be feeling His concern for this or that need, this or that person.

This is the source of prayer — the Spirit making intercession for the saints, who know not what to pray for as they ought. This is "praying in the Holy Ghost."

But this response leads to something else of great importance. For if God shares a burden or need which is on His heart with us, does He not already intend to fulfill it? More than that, has He not *already* fulfilled it in His sight, where past and future are one?

The best evidence that he *has* already fulfilled our need is the statement that before there ever was sin and need, there was already the provision of the Saviour (I Peter 1:20). That is God's upside-downness to our material sight — the supply provided before the need!

Paul says that Adam was "the figure of Him that was to come" (Romans 5:14). How can the fallen· Adam be a type, a figure, a pointer to a redeeming Adam? Because God is forever the Positive that swallows up the negative, just as mortality is swallowed up in life. Wherever there is a negative on earth — a have not, a need, a weakness, an unsolved problem, a sickness — His unchangeless character of perfect love *necessitates* His provision of the supply, strength, solution, health.

Love is always a debtor (Romans 1:14). It *must* move in and pay its debts of self-giving service. And God *is* love; therefore, the full supply is not in doubt.

"Before they call, I will answer," was God's word to Isaiah. His word is just the same today.

FAITH CHANNELED

Why, then, do we have these problems, these needs at all? Because human redemption is mediated through human agency — first through God's Son, and now through His sons. *So God puts us in tight spots to channel His creative faith through us.*

Our calling upon God in prayer is merely the evidence that He has stirred us into action. The answer is already there with Him, before we call. Now, as our calling moves on to the act of faith, God has His human agent in gear through whom He can channel the answer. It is never *our* need or problem or weakness, any more than it is *our* supply or *our* solution. Both are His. We are merely the human agents through which supply can reach need.

One more point. What about unanswered prayer — often in cases of illness, or concerning the unsaved, sometimes in material things?

UNION THROUGH GRACE

The whole point is: Whose prayer is it? The supplication of the Spirit through us, or our own?

Let us boldly say that it is *His* supplication, for the whole revelation of the union through grace is that He thinks, wills, sees through us in our normal daily lives.

Well, then, when we pray, we should say, "Lord, I am boldly interpreting this need as an evidence that you have the supply already on the way. I believe it. I receive it. Thank You."

Then, if the supply doesn't come as we expect, whose business is it? Obviously His. Leave Him to mind His own business.

If God wishes to appear a failure to the natural eye, let Him do so! He did at Calvary. Don't take back what you committed to Him as your concern. Don't accept from the Accuser blame for apparent failure or for apparent unbelief. Lots of us get tangled up and condemned at that spot. And don't take back a great heavy burden as if the final answer depended on how much you carried of it.

Leave your burden with God. Give the praise that really counts with Him — *not that which comes from the visible answer, but that which is based on naked faith.*

"Blessed are they who have not seen and yet have believed." "These all died in faith, not having received the promise." But they received enough by the faith which has the witness in itself to endure as seeing Him who is invisible, and to know, as the poet said, "On earth the broken arc, in Heaven the perfect round."

We, too, can have this experience. Today.

10. THE POWER OF ANOTHER WORLD

BY LEONARD RAVENHILL

Right at this moment a phenomenon, spiritual in character, is happening — in a place I could name, but dare not. Fifteen men, feared by demons, envied by angels, wondered at by men, are committed to a Spirit-designed assignment. These stalwart men of faith send out no prayer letters, solicit no funds and resolutely refuse to let their names be published. Their vigil is without precedent.

They have bought "gold tried in the fire." They have "eyes anointed with [divine] eye salve." Their souls are drenched with Calvary love. They are girded with might in the inner man by the Holy Ghost. How else could they have spent, as they have done, more than hundreds of consecutive nights of prayer for revival?

This is no prayer marathon, no itch for records — just passion for the lost. Such men are our modern Patons, Brainerds and Bounds.

In the deeper dimensions of prayer, in my opinion this is the deepest: *intercession.*

"Prayer is the simplest form of speech that infant lips can try," said James Montgomery.

True enough. But it is also so vast that it outranges all speech and exhausts every vocabulary. Eloquence is no value.

Moses stammered, but got prayer answered. Hannah opened not her lips, but triumphed in her intercession.

Can anyone with spiritual insight doubt that Hannah's

66

problem — barrenness — is ours today? If our altars are empty, what sense is there in our gloating over our Sunday school statistics, our colossal missionary pledges and our rally efforts?

Take barren Rachel. Obviously Jacob loved Rachel more than he loved Leah. She was beautiful to behold and doubtless loaded with jewels, as the custom of the day was. But these, or even Jacob's splendid devotion, offered no comfort. The "women's delight" was with Leah, for she had four laughing lads about her skirts. Men mocked and women shot out the lip at unfruitful Rachel.

I can imagine this forlorn woman met her husband one morning, her hair disheveled, her eyes more red with weeping than ever Leah's had been, and her voice coarse with groanings. Flinging herself at the feet of her lord, she cried with a piercing cry, "Give me children, or else I die!"

Oh, for thousands of Christians in America to cry this same petition. Oh, for thousands of pastors to be heartbroken about barren altars.

It is true that science has alleviated some of the suffering our mothers knew in childbirth. But science will never shrink the long slow months needed for child formation. As the coming babe encumbers the body of the mother, so the growing "body" of revival and soul-travail dislocates the church.

As a mother-to-be wearies more as the time of the birth draws near, often spending sleepless but not tearless nights — so the lamps of the sanctuary burn midnight oil while distressed, sin-carrying intercessors pour out their souls for a nation's iniquities.

As an expectant mother often loses desire for food in the interests of the one she will bear and denies herself certain things — even so a denial of food and consuming

love to lie quiet before the Lord seizes believers shamed by
the barrenness of the church.

As women in pregnancy hide from public gaze (or used
to), as the time of deliverance draws near — so those in
travail of soul shun publicity to seek the face of a holy God.

Revival comes as a result of the cleansed section of the
church bent and bowed in supplication and intercession.
Sickened at the sight of perishing millions, they wait —
perhaps days, weeks, months, in some cases (as with the
fifteen mentioned) years — until the Spirit moves *upon* and
through them; until heaven opens in revival blessing.

Let us not forget that women of the Bible who once
were barren later brought forth some of its noblest children.
Sarah, barren until ninety years of age, brought forth Isaac.
Rachel's cutting cry, "Give me children or I die!" was rewarded with the gift of Joseph — who in turn delivered a
nation.

Manoah's barren wife gave Israel Samson, who too was
a nation's deliverer. Hannah, sobbing, ignored the critical
Eli, prayed — and gave a nation the prophet Samuel. The
barren and widowed Ruth found mercy and bare Obed,
who begat Jesse, the father of David, of whose line came
our Saviour. Of Elizabeth, "well stricken in years," came
John the Baptist — of whom Jesus said, "Among them that
are born of women there hath not risen a greater . . ."

Shame of childlessness provoked these women. But what
mighty sons they bore!

For the present failure in the church the most pathetic
excuse is that we are barren of money. Rubbish. We lack
the supernatural.

E. M. Bounds was right in saying that when God wants
to do a job He looks for *a man.* "We are God's method.
What the Church needs today is men whom the Holy Ghost
can use — men of prayer."

Elijah was not an angel, nor was he sired by a seraphim. Elijah was not a demi-god. The divine record states that Elijah was a man — "a man of like passions as we are."

God had said that with a worm He would thresh the mountains (Isaiah 41:15), and in Elijah He did it. (Any worms around today?)

What was it that made Elijah, you ask? Faith made him all he became. And faith will do the same for us.

The resources that Elijah knew are available still — *plus* the finished work of the cross and the mighty power of the Holy Ghost.

We are not half-serious enough about the spiritual peril of millions. We are only "half there" if we merely want power to get a message over. Or to keep clean from sin.

What about stopping hell's legions?

How about invading heathen darkness?

Is it too much to believe that the Lord will endue men with a deep baptism with the Holy Ghost for this "end time" ministry that — even as Jerusalem trembled under the God-intoxicated men from the upper room in a matter of a few days — will shake nations in a matter of weeks?

We must repent of our unbelief — weep over our dryness — and take time to be holy.

About fifty years ago an attempt was made to assassinate Von Plehve, the Czarist Prime Minister. The plot failed, and Sazanov, the leader, was sent to a prison camp, one of the worst of its kind in Siberia. Prisoners there were flogged unmercifully. Sazanov schemed to show this crass wickedness to the world. Finally he hit upon a plan. When the guards were relaxed, he seized a can of kerosene, drenched himself with it and then set himself alight — so that the world gazing on one human torch might see past him to the incredible sufferings of his comrades.

All that for communism!

We Christians are not asked to burn like that. But we are offered the chance of becoming "a living sacrifice," of wielding a weapon of faith that will bring down on this spiritually stagnant age the power of another world.

Elijah prayed and the fire fell. He prayed and the people fell. He prayed again and the rain fell.

Brethren, let us pray, and let it be a prayer of intercession.

11. REQUEST WITH CONFIDENCE

BY DONALD E. HOKE

Christian Life Foreign Editor

It was Thanksgiving eve, 1947, at Columbia Bible College, and my heart was heavy with disappointment and unbelief, had I had the courage to admit it to myself.

Thanksgiving Day had been set as the deadline for the $50,000 being prayed in for the new women's dormitory just completed. As I left my office at 6 p.m. that evening, some $38,000 was still needed.

For weeks previous the President, Dr. Robert G. McQuilkin, had urged us of the faculty and student body to "pray the prayer of faith for this need." After the first few times, I had to admit to myself that his smiling, insistent exhortation to "pray the prayer of faith" irritated me. In my immaturity I argued, "Aren't all prayers, prayers of faith? I wouldn't pray if I didn't have faith would I?"

Thanksgiving Day festivities opened with worship and a message in chapel by President McQuilkin. His smiling face bore no trace of disappointment when he mounted the platform. After the usual preliminaries, he reviewed briefly the need for the dorm, the tokens of guidance leading to its construction, and finally our weeks of prayer for this large payment.

Then, his smile broadening, he announced that as of that moment the entire goal had been met. Late the night before visitors from the north had presented him with a check for $50,000 for the needs of the college!

That day a new horizon of understanding concerning prayer and faith began to open for me. I began to under-

71

stand that there's a qualitative difference between "the prayer of faith" and the wishful prayers customarily offered.

I came to realize that the three words, "prayer of faith," though mentioned only once in the Scriptures (James 5:16), knit together all of scriptural teaching on the vital subject of prayer and faith.

Ten years later God led me into more vital experience and understanding of this wonderful truth when the responsibilities of institutional leadership fell more directly upon me.

Japan Christian College had been going a year and a half. God had been blessing. In anticipation of the following spring's entering class, our board of directors — after reviewing the need, our meager resources, and God's will — was unitedly led to plan for purchase of an additional piece of property and erection of a large new dormitory. With confidence and thanksgiving we committed the matter to God in prayer.

Four days later a local amateur real estate agent came to my office and offered us five-sixths of an acre of land nearby at a fair figure. This was a miraculous first step in God's providence, because it had been almost impossible to buy suitable land in the neighborhood. The contract was signed and the college family began to look to God for the $8,000 needed by December 20.

In a remarkable way God sent in funds almost immediately. But December 19th dawned and darkened with $1,600 still needed.

The next morning when I rose to pray, I was confident that a messenger or cable would come, telling that God had miraculously supplied the need at the last moment before the 10 A.M. payment deadline. Sure enough, during the breakfast hour, a cable from America arrived telling of gifts for the new land.

But the amount was over $900 short of the goal.

With heavy heart I greeted the agent at 10 o'clock. He came in bowing and repeating polite phrases.

Would Professor Hoke kindly forgive him? It was a most regrettable circumstance, but it was unavoidable at this time. It seemed impossible to complete final transfer of title of the land at this date. It would have to be postponed approximately five days. And of course he would not ask for payment until the title was transferred. Would I kindly forgive this delay?

With singing heart I gladly forgave him — and voicelessly thanked God.

Saturday morning, December 22nd, the doorbell rang. At the door was a chaplain friend with news that he was to be transferred home over a month early. Under existing laws that he would be unable to sell his small, English car on the Japanese market, he had been led, in prayer, to give the car to Japan Christian College for disposal.

This meant that after proper lapse of time we could sell the car — and meet the payment deadline with funds remaining.

Thus, with rejoicing that God had answered our prayer of faith, final payment of $8,000 on the land was made.

In the years intervening between my first glimpse of understanding of the prayer of faith and my own experience of God's blessing and answer, God had wonderfully encouraged me through the life of James O. Fraser, pioneer apostle to the primitive Lisu people of western China (*Behind the Ranges*, by Mrs. Howard Taylor, published by China Inland Mission).

His work was painfully slow and difficult. After years of effort, there were only a few scattered Christians.

One day, with the burden of the Lisu tribes bearing heavily upon him, he knelt and claimed by faith in prayer that hundreds of Lisu families would turn to Christ. There, according to his testimony, he prayed the prayer of faith.

The burden lifted. In place of heartache and longing, there came quiet peace and thanksgiving. He was confident that God was answering.

Ten years passed before evidence of answer.

But when God visited Lisuland, Fraser testifies, "I believe it was January 12, 1915, that I was definitely led to ask God for 'several hundreds of families' from the Lisu. Some may say, 'Your prayer has at last been answered.' No! I took the answer *then*. I believed *then* that I had it. The realization has only now come, it is true, but God does not keep us waiting for *answers*. He gives them *at once*. (Daniel 9:23)."

I believe that the prayer of faith is entirely distinct from that general, exploratory prayer which it is necessary for every believer to offer in obedience to the commands of God in the Scriptures (e.g., pray "for kings and for all that are in authority . . ." (I Timothy 2:2, etc.)

It is definite, specific, and related to our primary responsibilities.

It is to be sought and offered for specific problems and needs in our personal lives, or in the ministries and responsibilities committed to us.

And it is concerning such specific prayers that most of the amazing commands and promises concerning prayer and faith in the Scriptures come to focus meaningfully.

Study of the Scriptures and the illustration of Fraser's and others' experiences as well as my own, have led me to four principles concerning this wonderful "prayer of faith."

1. *The prayer of faith is founded on knowledge of the will of God.* It is not voicing one's wishful thinking in prayer. It is not a broad, general, hopeful petition, prefaced with the usually misinterpreted phrase, "if it be Thy will . . ." Such expression is often excuse for unbelief, for failure to ascertain the will of God, or for unwillingness to pay the price of agonizing, importunate, Gethsemane intercession.

The prayer of faith must be preceded by (1) Insistently seeking to know God's will through the searching of the Scriptures, and (2) Earnest prayer for guidance to this vital knowledge.

Norman Grubb, Director of the Worldwide Evangelization Crusade, well taught in the school of prayer and faith, outlines the procedures followed in their mission concerning this vital point in a significant little booklet entitled *Touching the Invisible.* After the burden of leadership fell upon him, Grubb relates that God led clearly to his meeting with the mission staff every morning for prayer concerning the future of the world-wide work of the mission. Together, *before asking God for any need of the mission* (whether financial, personnel, the opening of a new field, or other), they sought earnestly to know the will of God concerning that problem. They examined the circumstances, the facts, the related factors, and earnestly searched the Scriptures for principles of guidance.

Grubb testifies that every single prayer, offered in faith after they had come to this knowledge of God's will, was abundantly answered.

2. *The prayer of faith acts in obedience to the Word of God.* Once the prayer of faith has been offered, one may not loll indolently waiting for God to answer. There will be acts of obedience, works requiring strenuous effort, intense spiritual conflict with the enemy of our souls who opposes any new step for God. But in it all will be quiet confidence that God has promised and will answer.

What are some acts of obedience that the Christian may be required to do when he prays the prayer of faith?

They, of course, vary with the petitions and the circumstances. If one is praying for the supply of a financial need, God may well require that the individual first do all that he can. He must see that he has been faithful in his stewardship, giving not merely a tithe, but beyond that in sacrifice. He may be required to give all that he can, however small that may be, as an evidence of his utter willingness to be the channel of accomplishing the will of God in this circumstance.

It was only through the hushed testimony of others that I learned that in frequent prayer and faith campaigns for the financial needs of Columbia Bible College throughout its history, its godly leader, Dr. McQuilkin, had often emptied his own bank account. He had on one occasion even mortgaged his own home. Only thus could he face God with the confidence that he had done all that he could, however small that might be — in order that, confidently, God might be expected to do His greatest.

3. Having obeyed God to the fullest understanding, *the prayer of faith then rests in the promises and faithfulness of God Himself*. The experience of Abraham is a glorious encouragement at this point. He waited long years in vain for a son. Old age robbed both him and Sarah of their reproductive powers. Yet God had promised them a son. And "it is written that Abraham against hope, believed in hope, that he might become the father of many nations . . . And being not weak in faith, he considered not his own body now dead when he was about a hundred years old, neither the deadness of Sarah's womb; he staggered not at the promise of God through unbelief; but was strong in faith giving glory to God; and being fully persuaded that what he had promised he was able also to perform" (Romans 4:18-21).

In other words the one who truly prays in faith simply rests in the promise of God.

4. A final encouragement to me has been the principle that *the prayer of faith grows*.

Once he has proved God in the prayer of faith, God calls his child, I believe, into trusting Him for even greater and greater things for His glory.

George Muller, a man whose life was marked by remarkable answers to prayer, testified that through sixty years his faith had steadily grown. Shortly before his death he said, "Today, if it were the will of God, I could as easily trust God for a million dollars as I could have trusted Him for a few rolls for breakfast in the early years of our orphanage work."

The implications are obvious. God does not trust His power, His honor, and His reputation to a neophyte. God will first prove us in little things before He entrusts to us greater things. He asks us to believe Him for small things before He gives us the conviction concerning His will to pray the prayer of faith for a greater thing.

Today God is longing to lead His servants out into prayers of faith to accomplish His purposes. Well over one billion of the world's population, approaching possibly a billion and a half, have never yet heard the name of Jesus Christ. The church is as weak and struggling, incapable of standing alone in many countries. In so-called Christian countries like America the glory of God burns dim, while drunkenness, immorality, and godless materialism flame out.

Prayer is the answer.

But such prayer must be not haphazard, hopeful expressions of personal desire, no matter how good.

The prayer of faith, as God has revealed it to me, is based upon conviction of the will of God, voiced with confident expectation that God will do what is asked. It is voiced in certainty that this petition is the will of God, that His promise therefore will certainly be proved true, that "whatsoever we ask according to His will, He *will* do it" (I John 5:14).

Such prayer doubts not at its circumstances, but rests with confidence in God's faithfulness and God's promises, and gives thanks until the answer comes.

12. LOVE IS THE ANSWER

BY GLADYS M. ROSE

Is there someone with whom you have talked until you can talk no more, and prayed for until your prayers seem old?

Have you been telling the Lord about an unsaved husband or wife, an unsaved son or daughter, a friend you have tried to win for many days — or a person who has harrassed you on your job for your Christian stand? Yet the skies are as lead. God seems not to hear. Nothing happens.

Love may be the answer to your problem.

An overwhelming flow of love can solve problems as nothing else can. A love that comes not from your own human incapability, but straight from the heart of God, as your spirit communes with His.

This is prayer of deeper dimensions.

About two and a half years ago a tragedy came to our Christian home which could have resulted in the loss of two souls. Our parents had raised the family to love God, and had taught us in the light of His Word. Even at a time when the mother questioned the existence of God, she had prayed that He would help her raise her children to become good adults. But one of the daughters, who had been saved and had known the presence of the Holy Spirit in her life, fell in love with a young Roman Catholic boy.

Realization of the divided home that would result and the grief in store for the daughter wounded the parents' hearts deeply. But they did not order her to break the engagement. They did not cry or fuss or threaten. They prayed.

And as prayer was made, our little family banded together and accepted this Catholic youth with open arms. From the moment he set foot into our house on the dreaded day when he was brought to meet the family, we offered our fears to Jesus and allowed the love of the Spirit of God to flow from us directly into his heart.

We loved and prayed, and loved some more.

No changes took place overnight. Hours of agonizing prayer were spent, and days of loving thought — pondering what to do and dreading the results of a bond between our girl and someone of a different faith.

Mother never spoke to her daughter on the subject unless she felt led of the Spirit. Even then, the words seemed to fall short of their destination. But Mother never forgot to love.

As we continued to pray for the salvation of him whom God had placed in our hands, our family tie drew tighter.

Love does not mean unconcern. It does not suggest that there is no need of prayer. It does not mean that agony — sometimes dread — is not felt.

It did lead the mother, in this case, in final desperation to yield all to God.

"God, do anything. Just don't let my daughter leave Your care."

God heard the cry of this soul. And He took her at her word. The mother herself was called upon to undergo suffering — seemingly unrelated to the need — out of which the victory could be won. An operation became necessary.

Today the young Catholic man testifies that the love shown in the family during the ordeal of the mother's operation opened his eyes. At last he could see the difference between salvation and religion. One Sunday morning he knelt at the chair from which he had been listening to the simplest and most beautiful love story ever told, and gave his heart to Christ.

That morning was worth everything we had suffered.

LOVE'S EXPRESSION

How is love expressed?

Principally through little things.

In this situation, it was the remembering not to argue one person's point over another's on religion.

It was remembering to smile and treat him like a human in his own right, not like an outcast sinner.

It was the thoughtfulness to do little helpful things in the everyday tasks of life that convinced this unbeliever of his need for Christ.

This was Christ's example also. He refused to allow the multitude to return home hungry after a day of listening to His voice on the mountainside. His love for them was manifest in His concern about their need for food. The disciples were too selfish for His attention to think of this.

Christ's Sermon on the Mount is compacted with exhortations to do the little things. "Walk the second mile." "Turn the other cheek." "Blessed are the peacemakers." "Give to him that asketh thee." I am sure Christ would want us to "give to him that asketh not," as well. He certainly set this example Himself.

"Love suffereth long . . ." Did not Christ stop in hostile territory and place His reputation in jeopardy to talk to a sinful woman about her soul? This was love.

Is this life-giving flow of love yours?

If you are burdened by the presence of an unsaved soul in your family, and prayer has been unavailing, consider.

Has God placed this stray child in your midst for you to love, as you pray — that, perhaps, at the same time, you may grow spiritually as you could in no other situation?

Think of the fruit tree. As spring approaches, the sap begins to rise from the roots through the trunk until it reaches the upmost branches. There, eventually, it bursts forth in perfect fruit.

COMPELLING INFLUENCE

Even so, can the Holy Spirit flow through you and cause you to blossom with the fruit of the Spirit — which begins with love. Respect for your loved one as an individual in his own right — respect for your husband or wife as a revered member of the home — is compulsive. This, along with the fruit of love, brings changes thought impossible.

Has not God promised that He will do abundantly above what we can ask or think — "according to the power that worketh in us": the power of a Spirit-filled life. "By this shall all men know that ye are my disciples, if ye have love one to another."

And love should not be limited to family or immediate friends. Love is the answer to the world's problem.

In the first church the Christians' love for Christ compelled them to "go forth and preach everywhere." Their worship was simple and sincere, their main task that of winning souls. Very few were leaders, or in "full-time" service. Most of them simply made the gospel message the theme of their lives as they went about daily jobs. Persecution only fanned the flame. It wasn't until Constantine made Christianity popular and heathenism began to enter the church that this great missionary movement diminished.

Today, in a world in which religion is considered a person's own business, love is still the compelling factor. Little things can influence society more than sermons.

One night at a restaurant the waitress, apparently quite tired, mixed our order. It would have been easy and very human to retort indignantly, or just to show our disgust by our actions. But it was so much sweeter — and almost fun —

to smile and make a light matter of it, even though it meant eating something not requested.

Another time, at college, it would have been less difficult to take someone's dry clothes from the automatic dryer and lay them on top so as to put my wet clothes inside. But it was more thoughtful — and much more satisfying — to fold the towels and take them to the person, mentioning with a smile that they were dry, so I had taken them out.

These things are not always convenient to remember.

But a true desire to love and to win reminds you of your duties even in seemingly unimportant little instances like these. Some things are not wrong if forgotten, but they are pleasant if they are remembered. And they make an impression on the life of an observant sinner. Your interest in small things concerning him will convince him of your interest in his soul.

This prayer of love can accomplish many things.

It can mend broken homes — and broken hearts.

It can save souls — and encourage those already saved.

It can bind friendships — and create friendships.

And love does not only bring results. It rewards the one who uses it — or allows God to use it through him.

Love, if genuine and sent from God, may be the answer to your prayer — and another's need. Your love for him is your highest prayer to God.

13. DO YOUR PRAYERS PLEASE GOD?

BY A. W. TOZER

Many prayer meetings are being called these days. And no wonder, for the need is great. But if my observation is correct much effort is wasted; very little comes of them.

The reason is that motives are not sound.

Too many praying persons seek to use prayer as a means to ends that are not wholly pure. Prayer is often conceived to be little more than a technique for self-advancement, a heavenly method of achieving earthly success.

Every kind of personal religious project these days is being made the object of prayer.

Some of these projects are unscriptural, or at least extra-scriptural, and many of them have no higher motive than to relieve the promoter of the unpleasant task of earning an honest living and to enable him to float about the world at the expense of the hard-pressed saints. Yet he may circularize his mailing list begging for the prayers of God's people, and call prolonged prayer meetings to try to gain the blessing of God upon activities God did not originate and will not own.

The Scriptures are very clear about the place of prayer in the economy of God.

Prayer was practiced by every believing soul from righteous Abel to John the Revelator, and it has been the vital breath of the church through the long centuries of her struggle on earth. Of prayer, properly understood, hardly too much can be said. This piece deals with prayer that is improperly understood and wrongly used.

The Scriptures are clear about the potency of prayer.

"The effectual fervent prayer of a righteous man," wrote the inspired James, "availeth much." With this the whole Bible and Christian experience agree: *Prayer is effective.* When it is not answered something is wrong.

The same apostle who affirmed the effective power of prayer admitted also that prayer is sometimes ineffective: "Ye ask, and receive not, because ye ask amiss, that ye may consume it upon your lusts."

In spite of the difficulties surrounding prayer it is still the highest activity in which a human being can engage. Knowing all about prayer and all about people our Lord said, "Men ought always to pray, and not to faint."

REASONS FOR FAILURE

This effort to discover the reasons for our leanness in prayer is intended not to discourage praying but to find the causes back of our ineffectual prayers and remove them. There is no virtue in continuing grimly to pray on when there are factors present that make our prayers of no effect. We should pray on, but we must pray aright or our prayers will continue to be fruitless.

We need only to listen to the average prayer to discover what is wrong.

Even in specially called prayer meetings where, it would be supposed, the most spiritual persons in a community are present, many of the prayers are little more than pious monologues on current events. They are suggested by the newscasts rather than inspired by the Spirit. They cover the earth like clouds without rain, promising much and delivering little.

To pray effectively we must want what God wants — that and only that is to pray in the will of God. And no petition made in the will of God was ever refused. "This is the confidence that we have in him, that, if we ask anything according to his will, he heareth us: and if we know that he hear us, whatsoever we ask, we know that we have the petitions that we desired of him" (I John 5:14-15).

Furthermore, to pray effectively we must pray within the context of the world situation *as God sees it.* Not what the world thinks about itself should influence us, but what God thinks about the world.

Prayer that slavishly follows the day-by-day development of world news may quite easily be wasted. Most world events as reported by the various news media are like ping-pong balls being batted back and forth. They are lively enough, they make an attention-getting racket, but they lack significance.

Surely the God who presides over history knows how few things matter. But He knows also what things *do* matter; and if we are spiritual enough to hear His voice He will lead us to engage in the kind of praying that will be effective.

For some years I have had a growing conviction that the world situation as God sees it presents two major goals to be reached by praying people, two objects at which to aim our prayers.

One is *that the glory of God be seen again among men,* and the other *that the church be delivered from her present Babylonian captivity.*

For several generations the evangelical Christian world has run on hearsay. We look back pensively to the Fathers who met God in brilliant and satisfying encounter. We quote them lovingly and try to draw what spiritual nourishment we can from the knowledge that the High and Lofty One once manifested Himself to wondering men. We pore over the record of His self-revelations to men like Abraham, Jacob, Moses and Isaiah. We read with longing hearts how once "the place was shaken where they were assembled together; and they were all filled with the Holy Ghost, and they spake the word of God with boldness." We read the stories of Edwards and Finney, and our hearts yearn to see again a shining forth of the glory of God.

OUR OBLIGATION

I believe we are under positive spiritual obligation to pray effectively till the present veil is torn away and the face of God is seen again by believing men.

The second object at which our prayers should be aimed is the restoration of the spiritual life of the church. We must continue to pray that she should cease her disgraceful fornication with the world and return to her first love and her true Lord. Her living has degenerated, her tastes have declined, her standards have sunk to the bottom. Nothing short of a radical reformation can save her. Only those with anointed eyes are able to see her plight and only those with Spirit-filled hearts can intercede for her effectively.

Now, even if we concentrate upon these vitally important items it is still entirely possible to ask amiss and gain nothing but leanness and utter disappointment. Why?

The problem is *self*. Selfishness is never so exquisitely selfish as when it is on its knees. Self is the serpent in the garden, the golden wedge in the tent of Achan, and it renders every prayer ineffective until it is identified and repudiated.

Self turns what would otherwise be a pure and powerful prayer into a weak and ineffective one.

I may, for instance, pray earnestly for the glory of God to be manifested to this generation of men, and spoil the whole thing by my secret hope that I may be the one through whom He manifests the glory.

I may cry loudly to God that the church be restored to

her New Testament splendor, and secretly dream that I may be the one to lead her in; thus I block the work of the Spirit by my impure motive. My hidden desire for a share of the glory prevents God from hearing me. So self, all bold and shameless, follows me to the altar, kneels with me in prayer and destroys my prayer before it is uttered.

It is possible to want the walls of Jerusalem rebuilt, but to want to be known as the Nehemiah who rebuilt them. It is possible to want the prophets of Baal defeated, but to dream of being the Elijah who stands dramatically on the mount to call down the fire for all the world to see. My strong desire for a new reformation within the church may be rendered void by my secret desire to be known as another Luther.

Did you ever pray that the armies of the Lord might win in the mighty struggle against the flesh and the devil and catch yourself daydreaming about riding up front in the open car when the grateful church stages a ticker tape parade to welcome the returning heroes?

If you are a minister, have you ever dreamed of a sea of eager faces hanging on your every word?

If you are a Christian businessman, have you ever let your mind wander over your mighty prayers for success in business, the dramatic answer, the proud testimony, maybe the tract with your picture on it?

Then you know what it is to be hit where it hurts worst; you know what it is to be attacked where you are most defenseless.

Too often we pray for right things but desire the answer for wrong reasons, one reason being a desire to gain a reputation among the saints. Long after every hope of getting on the cover of *Time* magazine has ebbed away from our hearts we may still harbor the unconfessed desire to get on the cover of *Christian Life*. That is, if the world will not appreciate our sterling worth, then the church will! If we cannot enjoy the reputation of being a great statesman or actor or ball-player we will settle for a big reputation as an unusual Christian. That is to desire flesh instead of manna; and God may send leanness to our souls as a result.

THE PERIL OF PRAYER

Nothing is so vital as prayer, yet a reputation for being a mighty prayer warrior is probably the most perilous of all reputations to have. No form of selfishness is so deeply and dangerously sinful as that which glories in being a man of prayer. It comes near to being self-worship; and that while in the very act of worshiping God.

What then shall we do?

We must deny self, take up the cross and count ourselves expendable.

We must cease to exercise the world's judgments and try to think God's thoughts after Him.

We must reckon ourselves dead to gain and glory and allow ourselves to become inextricably involved with the cross of Christ and the high honor of God.

Then our prayers will be something like this: *O God, let Thy Glory be revealed once more to men: through me if it please Thee, or without me or apart from me, it matters not. Restore Thy church to the place of moral beauty that becomes her as the Bride of Christ: through me, or apart from me; only let this prayer be answered. O God, honor whom Thou wilt. Let me be used or overlooked or ignored or forgotten.*

Prayer is still the greatest power on earth if it is practiced in the true fear of God. It is our solemn obligation to see that it is so practiced.